Unforgettable Ella

Unforgettable Ella

Susan Ryan

Xulon Press

Xulon Press
2301 Lucien Way #415
Maitland, FL 32751
407.339.4217
www.xulonpress.com

Xulon
PRESS

Edited by Xulon Press.

Illustrations: Elaine Ryan and Katie Ryan Donohue

Printed in the United States of America.

ISBN-13: 9781545624777

God Made the Horse
From the Breath
Of
The Wind
The
Beauty of the Earth
And
The Soul of an Angel

Source unknown

Contents

Memories

I stood with tears streaming down my face as I watched my best friend in the whole world leaving me. The hole in my heart was so large I was numb. I did not think it would really happen. I thought at the last moment something would intervene and stop it from happening. Even after she was gone, I couldn't move. My eyes were glued to the back of the horse trailer as it was leaving the driveway. She was gone. She was gone forever. The thought echoed in my brain.

Everyone from the barn was looking at me, not knowing what to say. I scanned their faces. Some had tears in their eyes while others reached out as if to try and stop the pain. I could not take it. I spun on my heel, grabbed my bike, and tore off for home. I had to find a place where I could spend my grief in private. I didn't know if I should scream or shake my hand at providence at how unfair it all felt. Why did this happen. I was given such an incredible gift only to have it taken away? It all just felt so unfair.

I crept into the house trying not to be noticed. I was making a beeline for my room when my mom called to me. "Hey Nicole are you alright?"

"Yeah, Mom, I'm fine," I said, but it was far from the truth. I was not okay. I just wanted this pain to go away. It was eating me alive.

"After you finish packing for college, we would like to take you out for dinner," she called after me from her art studio.

"I don't know if I'm really in the mood to go out, Mom." I was angry at her insensitivity. "Ella just left, remember?" I said, trying to keep my voice steady.

The mantra "She is gone" that had started echoing in my head rose up again, and the tears started to stream down my cheeks.

My mother came into the room and embraced me. I grabbed her fiercely, holding onto her and letting the grief I felt pulse through me. Then her words slipped over me as she said, "Ella was a great gift, something special. You must take what she has taught you and let it strengthen you. She allowed you to see the importance of so many things, such as determination, patience, love, loyalty, and courage. I know that you did not think I cared for Ella, but I saw how she made you stretch and grow. For that I will always be grateful. Remember when God shuts a door, He always opens a window."

The words were well meant, but all I could feel was my grief, and I muttered, "Yes, Mom." I closed my ears as she continued on with soothing words about Ella.

"The plan was always to sell that horse. You needed to sell her or else your chances of going to college and making a better life for yourself would not have been possible." I don't know if she was trying to console me or herself. I just hung onto her and let myself cry.

I am sure she thought that would ease the pain I was feeling. I loved my mother, but she just did not get it. To her, Ella was an extravagance that she thought I would outgrow. To me, Ella was my partner that my small world revolved around, and now that world was crashing in on me. I gently pushed away from her and said, "I just need to be alone." She squeezed my hand and left me to myself.

I shut the door to my small, cramped room and sat on the bed. It wasn't my mother's fault. She had her own problems. She didn't understand, and I did not have the ability to make her. She had always distanced herself from that part of my life.

I had a passion for horses. They were my life. She could not possibly understand why it would hurt so much to sell Ella. "After all, it was just a horse," she would say, "You can get another one later on once you have your life settled.

To me, Ella was my nearest, dearest friend. She would have done anything I asked of her. All of the best times of my life were shared with her. Together we had been through good times and bad, victories and failures. I would never forget her.

Eventually I stood up and looked around my room. There were half-packed bags here and there and clothes strewn all over. I picked up a bag and put it on my bed. Then I wandered over to my dresser to get the rest of my sweaters. I took them all out of the drawer and bundled them up in my arms. Once I had taken everything out, I looked back into the drawer. That is when I saw it laying in the bottom of the drawer. My arms went limp, dropping sweaters to the floor.

I stood looking at it. With a shaking hand I picked up the old photograph. It was a picture that I hadn't seen in years. In the picture was a tiny foal. The foal was dark and wet, and it had a beautiful white blaze on its head and one small white sock. The foal had a bright and curious expression that showed her intelligence. The foal's mother stood, nosing at her new creation. A petite girl with dark brown hair was cradling the little horse in her arms. The girl looked absolutely overjoyed.

I threw the bag off the bed and sat down again while still looking at the picture. So many memories were rushing back into my mind, one tumbling upon another, creating vivid pictures of friendship, warmth, pain, and love.

Frank

Our family had been living with our grand-mother ever since we lost everything. The family business had failed and my father was determined to climb out of the debt that hung over his head. It was awfully hard on the family. The whole way of life my family had known was gone.

Now our family of four was crammed into a small two bedroom house, living with my grandma. I didn't even have a room. I slept in the three-season porch that was attached to the side of the house where the nights got terribly cold before they insulated it. My dad did get on his feet again, but because he was determined to pay all the debts, there was absolutely no room for luxury.

I became a dreamer because of all the family troubles and the thing I dreamt about was horses. I read every book in the library I could get my hands on and I poured over magazines that had anything to do with horses. I would watch any TV show that had a horse in it. I learned as much as I could about them without actually touching them. The only good thing about my family's situation was that we were forced to move in with grandma who lived next door to Frank. Frank owned two horses that no one paid much attention to.

Our neighbor Frank called his horses "pasture ornaments." They had a nice large pasture with plenty of water and a small barn they could go in and out of as they pleased. The most exercise they had was dropping their heads down to eat. No one rode them. He had bought them for his children, but they had grown up and moved away. The horses were never given any real attention. Their manes and tails were full of burs, and their coats had a deep layer of dust on them.

I used to just sit and look at them. To me, they were wonderful. I started to feed them handfuls of grass. As they got used to me, I would spend long afternoons in their company. On those warm summer days I would make daisy chains and dream about great equestrian feats as the horses grazed.

Then one day I was caught in the pasture petting them. The owner called out to me, "Hey, what are you doing in there?"

I knew he was the owner and I had no right to be in the pasture with his horses. He called out again. I was about to run, but something inside of me had me walking in his direction. I started toward him with determination. He looked surprised but not angry. I explained to him that we were the family that had just moved in next door. I continued that

I had noticed no one seemed to care for the horses and asked if I could please care for them and maybe ride them. He looked down at me and said nothing for such a long time that I started to fidget. I was just thinking that I had gotten myself into trouble.

He then tilted his head and squinted at me and said, "You must be Nicole. Your grandmother told me about you. She said you are just plain horse crazy. I will talk with her and your parents, and I am sure we can figure out something."

God bless my grandmother. She had eased the way for me, and I was sure she would deal with my parents. For my twelve-year-old heart, that was a dream come true. After Frank had talked with my parents and, with the help of my grandmother, I was given the OK to ride. That day started a great friendship. I was in need of a friend.

Moving to the country and the circumstances that had led to it had left a rather large hole in me that I did not really understand. I had left all my old friends behind. School was not going to start for a whole three months, and the only person close to my age was my annoying younger sister who was afraid of horses. I was sure that this was going to be the worst summer of my life. Now all of that had changed. I had made a deal with Frank, and his wonderful half-wild horses were now a part of my summer.

The deal was made. I had to ride at my own risk and could continue to ride if I did a few chores around the barn. Cleaning the barn and tack was something I was sure I could do without much problem. Taking care of the actual animals was going to be a whole new experience. All I knew about horses had come from books and magazines, so this was taking it to a whole other level. Frank showed me around the small barn and the shed where he kept the tools, feed, and odds and ends. There was a small room where he kept the tack. He said he was not sure if any of it still fit the horses any more since they had become quite fat.

After the short tour I was eager to start riding. Frank showed me where the lead line and halter were placed. Each horse had a hook on the front of their stalls where they were kept. I grabbed the halter and lead line off the hook, impatient to get started.

Frank told me to hide the halter and lead rope behind my back until I got close enough to put a rope around their necks. With that bit of advice, I headed into their pasture to catch them. They did not pay much attention to me at first. I had spent so much time in the pasture with them that they were not afraid of me.

"Nicole," Frank called after me, "They can be hard to catch." Then he leaned on the fence to watch.

His advice was wonderful but not nearly enough. I had my head full of hope and dreams of galloping across open fields. The reality of that first encounter proved to be far different than what I had dreamed. The horses were not wary of me because I had spent time with them in the pasture giving them large handfuls of grass. But, I had never tried to put a halter on them. I got pretty close to them and thought, *No sweat; this will be easy.*

I could not figure out what Frank had been talking about when he told me to hold the halter behind my back. But I would soon find out. I walked straight at them. When I took the lead rope and halter from around my back their heads came up from eating and their eyes widened until I saw the whites around them. Their noses flared wide open and they snorted loudly. They ran from me as if I had taken a gun from behind my back. I thought Frank was going to bust his guts; he was laughing so hard. I had no idea what to do. If I made a quick move to grab them they just dodged me and took off again. This went on for about twenty minutes before Frank gave me another bit of advice.

"I think you should get some grain from the feed room and entice them into their stalls. I will help you," he said wiping tears of laughter from his eyes.

I was totally humiliated but determined. So, I marched over to him and he led me into the barn. We filled a pail with feed and swished it around so that it made the noise that let the horses know we were putting feed into their dinner bowls.

"You do not need much, just a handful. These greedy little buggers will come when they know there is food," Frank said.

True to his word, they came in to see what we were doing. While they checked out their feed pans, he closed the door on them. He said to me, "I think you better start with this one. She is not as hard to handle as the other."

"What are their names?" I asked.

"Well the dun mare here is Dusty Rose, and the chestnut gelding is Rebel." he replied.

"Figures," I said.

I grabbed the brushes, which were not much cleaner than the horses, and ran them over Dusty's body. She was a pretty golden dun color with a red stripe that ran down the center of her back. She had a half star on her forehead and her muzzle was soft and gray. She was a little nervous when I started to run the brush over her but seemed to settle down as we became used to each other. When I did something she did not like, she would pin her ears back against her head to let me know what she thought of my efforts.

Frank explained to the best of his ability how to brush and clean her feet out. The more I brushed her, the more the dust came to the top of her coat. Dusty was a good name for her! It had been years since anyone had really given her a good brushing. She had burrs in her mane and tail. Try as I may, I could not figure out how to get them out without her pinning her ears at me. Frank said, "Skip that for now." I did as he said, but was determined that I would come back later and get those nasty things out of her mane. I wanted her to be beautiful. I was sure there was a book at the library that had instructions on how to groom a horse and get all those sticky burrs out. Frank explained that the only time they were handled much was when the farrier came to attend to the horses feet.

"I am afraid you are going to have to ride her bareback. I do not know how to put a saddle on her." *Talk about the blind leading the blind* I mused. Frank continued in his apologetic way, "My kids did all the riding. Most I did was walk around a little on them and pay the bills. I am happy you have taken an interest in them, but I will be of little help in telling you how to ride. Let's see if I remember how to put the bridle on her." After many attempts we finally got her bridled. I made a note to myself to find a book on how to tack up a horse and ride at the library. My book list was getting longer and longer.

First Ride

The moment had come. I was going to ride a horse all by myself. I have to admit I was a little scared, but excitement overruled my fear. I summoned up my courage and took a deep breath determined to get on her. She was not a large horse standing at fifteen hands, but I was only five feet, four inches tall and had no idea of how to get on her. Frank suggested that I ride in the pasture until I got the hang of it. That seemed like a wonderful idea. I would do just that as soon as I figured out how to get on her. On my first attempt I moved her as close to the fence as I could get her. Then I prayed to God she would not move as I tried to slip on her back.

That did not work very well. Every time I tried to get my leg over her she would move just enough that I could not reach her. This went on for quite a while until Frank took pity on me and held her so she would not move—much. Finally, I grabbed a handful of mane full of determination that I would get on her this time. The ground looked pretty hard as I looked down from my perch on the fence.

Then, I took the leap of faith and it happened. I was finally on her. I just sat there with the reins in one hand and a handful of mane in the other. I released the breath I was holding and thought, *What do I do now*?

Frank showed me how to hold the reins and shared with me all the knowledge he remembered his kids telling him. "Don't hold the reins too tight but not too loose either. I think she neck reins so hold the reins in one hand, which is good for you since you have a death grip on her mane." I laughed but did not let go. Frank then tried to teach me how to direct the horse by moving the reins. "Now to put on the brakes, you need to pull back on the reins and say "Whoa"! That's about all I have to give you. From here on you are on your own. Oh yeah, when you want to go forward, tell her to walk and give a little kick."

I am not sure how long I sat there, but I finally took a deep breath, gave the command to walk, and gave her a little kick. She pinned her ears to let me know what she thought of all this business, but she took a step and I was on my way. I took a handful of steps, and I heard Frank yell, "Try the brakes." I pulled on the reins and said, "Whoa." She dutifully stopped and dropped her head to eat.

"She must have thought I said eat," I said to Frank.

Now what do I do? I thought. Frank, came to my rescue one more time. Give a pull on one rein until she gets her head up. It worked like a dream, but as soon as she felt me let go of the pressure on her mouth, the head went back down for another snack. This went on for a while until I figured out that as soon as I got her head up, I had to kick and say walk!

Frank had a nice, large pasture that was lush and green and ran along a creek. My first adventure on this horse consisted of following the fence down to the end of the pasture. In my mind, that fence line looked a mile long. I practiced the "walk and whoa" until I got her to quit diving her head to grab a bite to eat. She must have gotten tired of that because as we got to the end of the fence line and were turning to walk along the creek, she decided it was a good time to make a sharp turn, give a little buck, and dumped me on the ground.

As I lay on the ground, she took a good look at me and I'm sure she had a smirk in her eye. Then she promptly dropped her head to eat. I thought, *Well, that's not what I thought this was going to be like*. My dreams of galloping across the fields were pushed to the back burner for a while. I needed to learn how to stay on. I got up, brushed myself off, grabbed her reins, and started for the fence to practice getting on once again. I don't know how many times I fell off that day, but by the end of day I was pretty good at getting back on. By the end of that first ride I did finally get her to walk where I wanted her to go. My body was aching, but I had a deep satisfaction and sense of achievement that set me up for the next day. I walked her to the barn and brushed her off best I could. Then, I set off for the library.

That night after a good hot bath, I poured over the books I had checked out from the library. The best book I got was *The International Pony Club Manual of Horsemanship: Basics for Beginners.* That was me for sure. The book had everything I was looking for. It had chapters on how to select the proper horse for the beginner. I did not have any choice on the horse I would ride, but it was full of good information, so I read it. The one thing it did confirm was that you did not put a beginner on a half-wild horse. That was a chapter I was definitely going to keep away from my mother's eyes.

The other chapters on learning to ride, horse care management, general horse knowledge, tack, and turnout were things I wanted to make part of my new adventure on becoming an equestrian. What a long way I had before me, but the future looked bright. The book set it up step-by-step, and I was determined to take those steps. It was full of pictures, and I would spend hours trying to copy what I saw in those pictures. All the images showed a person riding with a saddle on the horse. That sure looked like a good idea-especially those wonderful stirrups for getting on.

The next day, as soon as my eyes opened I grabbed my Pony Club manual. I ate a small breakfast and made my way over to Frank's little barn. With my new book in hand I had new eyes for the barn. Things that I had not noticed before came jumping out at me. The barn had not had a good cleaning in quite a while. There was dust and cobwebs everywhere. I thought the least I could do was to put it back in order. I started with cleaning the stalls. They were not bad because the horses were only in them to eat and lived mostly outside in the lean-to. Next, I attacked the cobwebs and swept the floor. That took care of my morning.

In the afternoon I went back to the barn and looked in the small tack room to see if they had a saddle and girth for the horses. I was in luck. There was an all-purpose, English saddle with girth under one inch of dust just waiting for me. You could tell at one time someone had taken care of the tack room. There was a nice place for the saddle and bridle, a special place for the brushes, and a shelf with other barn items. The room was nice and tidy under all the dust. Someone had put everything in its place, shut the door, and forgot about it. There was a clock on the wall that had stopped working with its hands pointing at 3:33. The room had stood still in time just waiting for me to bring it back to life.

I went to work dusting everything off and putting new batteries in the clock. There was a treasure trove of items for horses. Some things were dried out and I had to throw them away, but most were in good shape and just needed a little TLC. I found some soaps and conditioners made for the saddle and bridle and got right to work cleaning them.

After I finished up with the saddle and bridle I was determined to get rid of the burr bushes in the pasture. I grabbed a shovel and small saw to cut them down with. They all seemed to be clumped together in a small area. I have no idea why the horses would even want to eat in that area. There must have been something that made the grass sweeter there because their manes were full of those burrs.

It was a much harder job than I had anticipated. My new number-one enemy were burrs. Why God created such horrid things I could not imagine. It took me most of the afternoon to get rid of them. I really did not mind the work. It was a wonderful summer day with big fluffy clouds in a blue sky that kept me out of the house and away from the endless, boring chores my mother always seemed to come up with. With a great sense of victory I dug out the last burr bush and added it to the pile for Frank to burn.

Tired, I leaned on my shovel, my eyes following the creek where the horses stood grazing under a tree. I announced to them that their days of neglect were over and I would make them beautiful again. They raised their heads to see what the fuss was all about, but soon lost interest and went back to grazing.

Dusty Rose

$\mathcal{D}$usty was next on my list. Those burrs in her mane had to be removed. I grabbed a small bit of grain to entice the horses into their stalls. This was a great trick Frank taught me. I grabbed the halter, took a good look at the pictures in the book, and did my best to figure out how to put it on Dusty's head as she was eating. I only had a small window of time to figure it out because once she was done with her grain, she had no patience for me. I got the job done and put her on the cross ties.

Now it was time to attack those burrs in her mane and tail. The best tip I got from one of my books was to start at the bottom of the mane and work upward, pulling the hair apart as you went while making sure you held the hair in your other hand so it did not hurt her skin. I had found an old radio that was set on a shelf near the cross ties and turned it on to the oldies station. I went to work on Dusty's mane and tail singing along with the music. She would pin her ears at me occasionally, but not once did she complain about my singing.

After I was finished, I stepped back to view my handiwork. The burrs were gone, but the mane looked like a frizzy mess. I took some water to it, and that seemed to help smooth it out.

The next thing I did was get the saddle and blanket and see if I could figure out how to put it on by looking at the pictures in the manual. Lucky for her I just could not quite figure it out. That whole summer I rode without saddle and half the time without a bridle too. I got to the point where I could grab a handful of mane and hop up on her back. Of course she never stood still, but I got real quick at getting up on her. Over the next few weeks I learned to walk, trot, canter and every once in awhile I would open her up to gallop. I was not a great equestrian, but I had learned to stay on even when she gave me her little bucks. She had other little quirks that helped me pay attention. One of her favorites was heading for low branches to skim me off her back, but I got good at ducking and eventually she stopped doing that.

I spent every minute I could at the barn that summer. If I was not riding or cleaning I would just lay on her back while she was grazing in her pasture and watch the clouds roll by.

I think she even began to like all of the attention I was giving her. When she saw me coming she would head to the barn to meet me. If she was out of sight in the far pasture I would whistle and she would come running for her treat.

One warm beautiful fall day Frank came and was watching me ride and said, "You have quite a way with her, and the barn looks good. I think you are ready to ride her outside of the pasture. There are some great trails over near the Sisters Woods that you can ride on if you want."

That is where I met Brad for the first time. Brad was on a tall, dark thoroughbred that he was exercising for a barn he was working at. He was jumping a small log that had fallen during a storm. It took my breath away to watch the two of them work. I just sat there on Dusty and watched him school that gorgeous animal. He finally noticed me and rode over to where I was watching. When he got close he said, "Don't you ride the same school bus I ride?" I was surprised he even remembered me.

"My name is Brad, what is your name?"

"I am Nicole. That is some horse you have there," I said.

He laughed and said, "He is not mine. He is just one of the horses from the barn I work at that the owner did not have time to ride. She asked me to ride him and work him on the trails. I guess he gets himself all worked up and tries to run away when he gets scared. So far, he has been good though."

"Where did you learn to ride like that?" I asked.

"Oh," he waved his hand and said, "Where I work, you have to learn to ride or you don't have a job. As riders go, I'm Okay but far from great."

"From what I saw, I was quite impressed," I said.

He ignored the compliment and asked if I would like to ride with him.

He knew all the trails so I followed him. As we were cantering along we came across a log that was in the trail. His horse went over it without even breaking stride. But Dusty, bless her heart, threw the brakes on and I went flying forward over her head. I somehow landed on my feet facing her with the reins in my hand. She stood looking at me with her eyes wide open.

"I guess she doesn't jump." Brad laughed."

"No, I guess she doesn't jump," I said.

"I can teach you both how to go over these little logs if you want," he offered.

I did not hesitate. "I am all for it if you want." So, we found a little clearing. He got off his horse that stood perfectly still, and found a large, ten-foot branch that Dusty could walk over. He had us walk toward it. I could feel Dusty tensing up under me and knew she did not want to have anything to do with this.

Brad encouraged me by saying, "Put more leg on her and look up."

I looked at him and said, "Put more leg on her? Where am I supposed to look?"

Just as we were getting near the branch she ditched out on me. I almost fell off as she did her sharp turn. With a handful of mane, I readjusted my seat with all the dignity I could muster and looked at Brad. He was holding back a laugh.

When he got himself under control he said, "Oh, let me explain what I mean. When I said put your leg on her I meant give her a little squeeze and maybe a little kick to keep her going. Look ahead of the branch; don't look down at it, or she will look at it also. That will make her ditch out at the last second. If you keep your eyes on where you want to go she will follow. So, look beyond the branch to where you want to end up. Now try again. Make a big-enough circle that you can come at it straight through the middle." I did as he said and when I felt her tense up, I gave her a squeeze and a little kick and kept my eyes up and forward. She walked right over it. He had me go over it again and again at a walk, then at a trot, and then at a canter. By the end of the little lesson I felt braver, and so did Dusty.

That fall was filled with trail rides and short lessons from Brad. Dusty was going over the small logs on the trail without hesitation and that felt great. This made me want to learn about every aspect of riding even more.

One day Brad asked me, "Do you have a saddle for that horse?"

"I do, but the last time I tried it on her she was so plump that the girth would not go all the way around her. To be honest with you I have never put a saddle on a horse and am not sure how to do it."

"She looks like a different horse than the one you started to ride this summer. She is not so round, so maybe the saddle will fit. Let's give it a try," Brad said.

The very next day Brad showed up after school and showed me how to saddle Dusty. He was very patient. He explained that it had been a long time since she had a saddle on her back, and it might take her some getting used to. He told me the importance of where to put the blanket and saddle. It had to be in just the right place on her back, or it could make her very sore. He talked to me about how to rub her down after riding and the importance of a short bath that would take all the sweat marks off of her. He showed me how to clean the tack, and we talked about the importance of good horse management. He pointed out little things that might be dangerous for the horses and should be fixed right away. He gave me eyes to see things I had read about, but had not fully understood until I had someone show me.

The saddle took some time for me to get used to. I was used to riding bareback and preferred it. The saddle felt like it was in the way, but Brad said if I wanted to jump and learn dressage, I should learn to ride with a saddle. So I did.

Then one Spring day Brad showed up at Frank's small barn as I was saddling Dusty and said, "Hey, Nicole do you want to come to the barn and see my new horse Liam tomorrow?

The Equestrian Center

The Equestrian Center was the talk of our small community. I was extremely curious about what was happening in this magical place of equine events, and Brad had just asked me to go there. It was something I wanted to see more than anything. I had only been around my neighbor's backyard horses but was curious to see what the Equestrian Center was all about.

"Sure," I said like it was no big deal.

The farm was only a short bike ride from my home. After school I told my mother where I was going. As I was closing the door I heard my mother say, "You be careful around those animals and do not be late for dinner." "Okay Mom," I said quickly before she changed her mind. I hopped on my bike to meet Brad with no idea of the adventure that was about to unfold before me.

It was one of the first days of spring where warm sweaters and jeans were enough to keep out the cold. The sun warming my skin assured me that winter had lost its grip and was giving way to spring. The signs of the coming season were everywhere, whispering promises that ignited hope of new things to come.

As I reached the top of the hill I got my first glimpse of the farm. It was breathtaking. I had seen it from the window of our car but seeing it up close was very different. White fences seemed to run forever on perfect, lush green hills. Horses were everywhere in all imaginable colors and shapes. The barns were white with deep dark evergreen roofs. Rows of maple trees just starting to bud lined the long sloping driveway that spilled onto the perfectly manicured lawn. I do not know what I was expecting, but I had no idea a place like this could exist. It was intimidating, and I felt like an outsider.

I was just turning my bike around to leave when Brad came out of the barn waving at me. "Just put your bike over here. I cannot wait for you to see my boy," he said, warmly and excitedly as he waited for me. When we walked into the equestrian center it was buzzing with activity. People and horses were heading in all directions.

"Let's take a shortcut through the lounge," Brad said as he directed me toward a door on the right. The lounge was nicer than my home. It included a full kitchen with dining table and an office with large comfy couches that faced a wall of windows that overlooked the indoor riding arena.

"Wow," was all I could say. I had never seen an indoor riding arena. I just wanted to stare at all the activity that was going on in the arena, but Brad was on a mission and stopping and gawking at everything was not part of it.

"He's down this way. Let's go!" he said. He was really excited to show me his new horse. He took my hand and led me down the rows of stalls that housed these beautiful animals.

"It seems wrong to call this just a barn," I said as my head swiveled from side to side, trying to take everything in. As we walked I noticed tack rooms where horse equipment was kept. Each horse had its own tack area that usually contained two saddles, bridles, lead ropes, halters, and best of all, a large tack trunk that had the owner's name on it along with the horse's name. There were also wash stalls that had hot and cold running water where you washed your horse down after riding. Next to that were areas where you could groom and saddle your horse. In each corner of the barn was a feed room where they kept the instructions for each horse's nutritional needs. There were also extra food and supplements and the schedule of each horse's routine in those rooms. Those feed rooms stood like sentinels over-looking the care of the horses. My own home did not have the organization this barn had. There was a place for everything, and everything was in its place.

I mumbled under my breath trying not to look to starstruck. "This place is huge and everything is so perfect. Makes me want to be a horse."

Brad gave me a gentle nudge and said in a snooty voice "We do not think of it as just a barn. It is called an equestrian center that is set up for the purpose of accommodating, training, and competing. There is a full riding school and we even have our own blacksmith and a small tack shop with basics where you can get equipment repaired. Carol even opens it up for the local pony club to use," he said with a laugh.

I am sure Brad was enjoying how overwhelmed I was and rubbing it in a little because he was also proud that he worked in such a great place.

"Well, I can see you have arrived," I said imitating his snooty voice. Teasing him helped to hide the jealousy I was feeling. They should use you as a spokesman for this equestrian center," I teased. Brad gently gave me a push and we continued walking toward his horse's stall.

"How much farther is his stall?" I asked. I could not help peeking into each stall to look at these brilliant animals as we walked down the aisles. Each of the stalls had a small laminated card with the horse's name and the owner's contact and emergency information on it.

I stopped walking for a moment and inhaled deeply. The smells were intoxicating. There was fresh wood shavings, sweet hay, and best of all, the smell of horses—a smell only those who love the animal can truly appreciate. I could hear the muffled clip-clopping of hooves on the cement aisle on the other side of the barn. I could also hear the quiet chewing of horses eating hay and grain. It was so peaceful. I wanted to just stand there and let it sink into my soul.

"Hey, come on! Don't just stand there!" Brad urged. That is when I noticed a horse's stall without a name tag on it.

"How come this stall does not have a name tag on it? Wow, is she cute!" I said in the same breath, as I peeked into the stall. The horse was a deep, seal bay, almost black color. She glimmered in the sunlight that slanted through her window. She was fined boned with a delicate head and wide-set brown eyes that looked at me as I gazed at her. Her intelligent face seemed to say, "Stare at me all you like. I know I am something special." After she inspected me, she dropped her head to finish her dinner.

"Oh, that is Letty. She is new to the barn. That's why there is no information on her stall yet. She's green and in training. She is one of Carol's new favorites."

"Green?" I replied.

"Yes, what that means is that she is just learning to accept saddle, bridle, and rider. They started her off with lunging."

"What is lunging?" I asked.

Brad sucked in a deep breath deciding the effort he was about to put into his answer. "Well, basically, this is where a person stands at the shoulder of the horse with a long line attached to the halter or cavesson. The person then asks the horse to move away from him in a twenty-meter circle around him at a walk, trot, and canter. This starts training the horse to listen to and obey the handler. It also begins the process of getting the horse balanced. It teaches the horse to listen to your voice commands and to obey them. It should also train him to go forward when asked with a flick of the lunge whip," Brad explained.

I just stood looking at him not understanding what he was talking about. He looked at me laughed and said, "On the way out of the barn, let's look in the riding arena and see if someone is lunging their horse. Then you can see what I mean."

"Sounds good to me," I replied. Anything that kept me there longer sounded great. This was a world I never knew existed and it was opening my eyes to endless possibilities.

"I bet the horse I ride never even saw a lunge line. I think someone just got on her one day and said, 'Go.' No wonder the poor thing is so cranky; she does not know any different."

"Well you can always come here while I am working and watch the trainers here and pick up some pointers if you want," Brad offered.

"Do you really think it would be okay?" I asked.

"I will ask Carol and see what she has to say," Brad replied.

"Carol takes starting a horse very seriously because it is the foundation for the job it will do for the rest of its life. Carol always says 'a good foundation, a safe horse. Letty is a natural and takes to training with ease. She seems to trust people and stays calm no matter what she is asked to do," Brad explained.

"She is absolutely adorable!" I said singing her praises.

All I wanted to do was look around, but Brad continued on toward his horse's pen. Brad's horse was kept in a small paddock behind the barn that had access to a pasture. "This place is just so perfect! You're lucky you can keep your horse here. How do you afford the board?" I asked.

"Well, I worked out a deal that pays for his board. Here we are! This is him! This is Liam!" He said as if he were presenting a king.

Liam

The first thing I heard as we came closer to the paddock was a deep, rich nicker that washed over me in welcome, warming my heart. I had never heard a horse nicker. Whinny yes, but this deep, obviously warm emotional sound was something new. I asked Brad about it. He explained that horses make that sound to others in their herd as a "Hello, good to see you."

"I guess he has decided that I am one of his herd. He makes me feel real welcome," he said as he reached over the fence to rub his head.

I peered over the fence into the paddock. In it was a tall thoroughbred with a cute round pony next to him. The thoroughbred was a pleasant seal bay, almost black with a broad chest and straight powerful legs. He must have been beautiful once, but now he was a bag of bones. His coat was dull, and he looked all used up. As I came closer to the stall, I noticed that he seemed interested in me, and his eyes followed me closely as if he was saying "Who are you? Can I trust you?" Somewhere along the line he had seen hard times. I was not as impressed with Liam as Brad was, but it must be different when the horse belongs to you.

"What do you think?" Brad asked.

After all the buildup, I did not quite know how to answer him.

"Well, it is hard to say. He has good color, a broad chest, and a keen eye but, Brad, you can count every rib along his sides. It makes me wonder who could starve such a beautiful creature and why?" I felt bad immediately after I had said it; Brad seemed so proud of the horse, and I just totally trashed it. I looked into Brad's face to see if he was angry, but I didn't see any signs of anger.

"I know, but you should have seen him when he first came in. I wasn't sure he was going to live. We keep all the food he could possibly eat in front of him at all times. He always has a nice supply of freshwater and hay before him. He also has free access to a nice, green pasture during the day. I feed him a small amount of grain and vitamins three times a day. You would not believe it, but he actually looked worse when he first came to the barn. He will be beautiful again. I do not know his full story, but I have a real bond with him."

"He was a racehorse and a good one from the records I was able to find on him, but whoever owned him when he stopped winning must have stopped feeding him. Some race horses can have many owners throughout their career, some better than others. His last owner had put him up for auction knowing that he would end up as dog food. But, it was his lucky day because Carol saw him. She took a chance that she could bring him back to health and bid on him, saving his life. She isolated him on the side of the barn away from all the other horses to make sure he would make it. The veterinarian came and cleared his health and assured Carol that if she could get him to start eating that he could be used as a pleasure horse. He speculated that the horse had been drugged to keep him running and that she might be dealing with withdrawal and some pain issues at first."

"The first time I saw Liam, I have to admit that I didn't have much hope for him. He would stand in the corner of the corral with his head hanging down, not moving. I would come and clean out his area, and he would barely take notice of me. I would set fresh food in front of him, and he would look at me and seemed to say, 'Don't bother.' Then one day I found myself talking to him. I would pick the greenest grass I could find, and he would nose it, finally eating that out of my hand. I would come off and on during the day just to talk and keep him company and feed him grass. Then one thing led to another and I cleaned out his hooves, brushed his coat, and found myself talking to him about everything. I came to just like his manner and quiet way.

He is a tall horse but does not use his size to intimidate you. He seems to listen to every word you speak to him. I know it sounds crazy, but we have become buddies. I told him he had to start eating. Then one day he turned his head, gave me a hard look, swished his tail, and started to eat. I guess he decided to give life a second chance.

"After that he started to look for me and I could not keep enough food in front of him. He gives me a deep, rich nicker of welcome whenever he catches sight of me. He makes me feel special like we belong together."

"As he grew stronger, he started to pace up and down the fence line. I was worried he would run off everything he ate. Horses don't like to be alone. Especially Thoroughbreds. They are much like the Arabian breed, who are sensitive and become attached to those they perceive to be their owners. Whoever trained him must have really cared for him because there is a good richness of trust that runs deep in him that is true to his breeding. He has good manners and never even thinks of getting in your space. I was worried about his pacing and talked to Carol about him. She said to put High Tops in with him and see if that would calm him down."

"High tops is a retired hunter pony. He got his name from the four white socks that went above his knees and hocks. He is a cute thirteen-hand, two-inch, round, black-and-white pony that carried children around the ring and made them feel like champions. He had put up with and taught a large number of children how to ride and jump. He is retired now, and the thing he is best at is eating. He was just what Liam needed. They got along like old lost friends. They stick to each other like glue. Wherever Liam goes, High Tops is not far behind. They stand next to each other during the hot part of the day and gently brush flies off each other with their tails as they eat. When High Tops lays down to take a nap, Liam stands over him and keeps guard. They are quite the pair."

"Carol was watching how I took an interest in Liam and how he was responding to me. After she was sure he would live, she offered him to me on the stipulation that she had the first chance to buy him back if I ever had to sell him. She has a soft spot for these guys who work so hard and then get dumped. Look, they raced him so hard that both of his front tendons bowed." I looked to where Brad pointed on the horse's front legs. I could see that both front legs looked inflamed and way too thick to be normal.

"Oh, how awful. Is he in pain?" I asked quietly.

"I am sure it was extremely painful when it first happened. The veterinarian said because of where it happened he may not be lame, but the legs may never be quite as strong as they were before. So, no serious racing or jumping for this fellow. That's okay by me. I just want a trail horse and maybe do some dressage. Besides, I know he will be beautiful to look at again soon." Brad said.

My respect for Brad grew that day. There was a lot more to him than the average person. There was a kindness in him that you did not notice at first glance, but the way he lived his life made it shine.

"This is a pretty fancy place to keep a trail horse," I teased.

Brad replied, "Carol and I worked out the details of how I was going to keep him. I will let you know I got the better end of that deal. His registered name is Smooth Fleet. His great grandfather's name was Count Fleet, a Triple Crown winner."

"Whoa," I breathed.

Brad continued to brag on his new horse. "I was able to look up his racing record, and it shows that he has won a whole lot of money. However, they dumped him once he stopped making money. Carol promised him to me if I swore to care for him and bring him back to health."

"Who is this Carol person? She just gave you this horse?" I asked.

"Carol is the owner of the barn. She rescues ex-racehorses like Liam from time to time. She loves horses. She's awesome. As long as she sees that you are putting forth your best effort she is easy to get along with. I have to admit though, she makes you stretch. She sees things in people and animals that most do not see. It is not the questions or even the conversations you have with her but how you respond to the environment around you that she uses to measure what is inside of you. I believe that is why she is able to rescue horses and succeed. She has taught me so much about horses. She is a real stickler for details and expects you to give your best, but she has a real big heart. You just can't help but like her. I just can't say enough good about her. Sometimes I feel like she saved me right along with Liam," Brad said.

Life for Brad was not easy. His dad was a farmer who could barely keep a roof over his family's head. There was not a lot of room for love in his family and Brad was hungry for adventure and friendship. His good nature and zest for life made him fun to be around, but he had told me about the gangs at school that were always after him to join in. It was hard for me to believe that he even considered joining in such a thing as I looked at him standing there self-assured with a natural kindness that ran deep in his soul.

"That is amazing. If someone just gave me a horse, I don't know what I'd do!"

"Yeah, it surprised me, too. I'll show you the rest of place, but first I have to feed Liam," Brad said as he walked off toward the feed room. After his horse was fed Brad took me around the barn. All of the horses were well taken care of and in great shape. I especially liked the mare I had seen earlier. Letty was her name. She was my new dream horse. As I walked through those aisles I fantasized about being able to keep a horse of my own at this place one day. When Brad returned, I said, "Wow, this place is so great. You are really lucky, you know that? I'd give anything . . ." I looked around again without finishing my last sentence. I shouldn't get my hopes up.

I finally said, "I have to get home. Thank you so much for bringing me here."

He replied, "It was my pleasure. I'll walk you to your bike. Come on."

"No, I don't think so. It's all right." I walked away. I didn't want him to see that I was jealous. I shouldn't be, but I couldn't help it. He had everything I wanted. This world he was in was something I wanted so badly to be a part of. It tore me up to know that I would probably never get the chance.

Doors and Windows

*A*fter school I ran straight down to the old barn from the school bus. I didn't want to go into the house. I needed to think and the privacy of Frank's barn was the perfect place to sort out my thoughts. I wanted to dream about the Equestrian Center without any interference. I flipped on the radio joining in with the oldies singing at the top of my lungs. I was straightening the barn when I noticed Brad out of the corner of my eye standing there grinning at me.

"When did you get here?" I asked.

"Just long enough to hear you sing those last couple of notes. Now I know why your horse is so hard to catch" he grinned.

I just stood there looking at him thinking, *Why was he alway catching me at my worst?*

I straightened up and asked "What's up?"

"I came by to see if you would like to take a trail ride. Liam has recovered enough to start easy trail rides."

"Really?! Of course I do! Can I ride Dusty over there?" I asked.

"Sure, why not? I will wait here while you saddle Dusty and we can walk over together."

"Are you sure Carol won't mind that I bring her?"

"Why should she? It's a horse barn. That's a horse—at least I think it's a horse," he said, teasing.

"Hey, watch what you say. She is very sensitive about her looks." I said as I covered her ears.

Brad laughed, but I had come to love that little mare. I knew she was not that much to look at and she was very old, but we had come to terms with each other and I felt very protective about her. Over the summer I got her to the point where she looked neat and trim. She was no longer the fat, cranky horse that bucked me off every chance she got. That alone gave her merit in my heart.

"Let's go!" I said as I swung my leg over the mare.

As Brad and I started out toward his barn, I looked up and noticed that the sky was starting to turn gray and it looked like bad weather was coming in. When we got to the driveway the wind was starting to pick up.

"Just ride in the empty dressage ring while I get Liam," Brad said as he ran off to get his horse. I had never been in a dressage ring and did not really know what to do. I saw a rail in the middle of the ring and started doing large looping circles over it just like Brad had me work on in the field.

We started at the walk with a long rein. Then we worked up to the canter looping back and forth over the rail. Everything seemed to be going great when all of the sudden I could feel the mare tense up beneath me. The huge maples that were placed on either side of the driveway started to pitch and wave back and forth. "Take it easy, girl," I spoke gently to my frightened friend. Her head was high in the air and she was more alert than I had ever seen her. Suddenly, a paper bag whipped across our path. The mare reacted like it was a huge gigantic monster that was going to eat her and that's when all the fun began.

"Whoa!" I screamed as the mare started running for her life. I tried to pull her up but she started to buck. She leaped into the air and attempted to heave me off of her back several times before she succeeded in doing so. I was thrown through the air and landed heavily on the ground with a thud. I laid there dazed for a couple of seconds. Then, when the reality of what had just happened came back to me I turned onto my back. I saw Brad running over to me. He crouched down next to me. "Are you alright?"

"Yeah. I think so," I said as I took inventory of my bruises. No broken bones. Just a large dose of humiliation and a couple of bloody knees. "Nothing that won't heal."

"Boy, you sure ate dirt on that fall! I have never seen a horse buck like that in my life! Wow! You're sure you're okay? Don't move for a while," he said as he crouched next to me, looking worried.

"Well, I finally found something that my mare can do that impresses you," I said with a grin. Brad just looked at me and frowned.

"Really, I'm fine." I reached out to him to help me up. I could see a lecture forming in his mind, and I did not want to hear it.

"Don't worry, that is not the first time that mare has done this to me. I usually don't have an audience when she does it. Rotten little bugger," I muttered under my breath.

Then I stood up. "I better go get her before she decides to run home," I said as I tenderly rubbed at my bloody knees.

I looked up into the sky once more, and this time dark rain clouds were moving in. I knew it was time to head for home or I would be caught in the downpour. I grabbed Dusty's reins and looked her over. She looked fine standing there, but to be on the safe side I led her in a slow walk. That is when I saw the limp.

Brad came over and ran his hand down her right front leg. "No bumps or open wounds. She just probably landed on it wrong when she was bucking. You better ice it when you get her home just to make sure."

My humiliation melted away to worry as I saw my old friend limp. Though the limp did not look too bad, I would hand-walk her home and ice the leg.

Brad came alongside of me and offered to walk home with me, but I called him off saying, "I'm sure you have to finish your work before the rain starts."

"That is true," he said. "Can I stop by tomorrow and check on both of you? I'm sorry you fell off Dusty. You had some nice moments as you were working on those figure eights. Carol and I were watching from the barn."

I threw my head back and closed my eyes just as the first drops of rain hit my face. Humiliation started to burn through me. I had so wanted to make a good impression on this Carol person, and the first thing she sees of me is falling off my horse. I patted Dusty's neck and said to her, "At least you keep me humble." I gathered her reins to take the long, wet walk home.

"You're absolutely positive you are one-hundred percent okay, right?" Brad asked one more time.

"Well, maybe I'm only ninety percent," I said giving him a jab. "I'm fine. Go finish your chores. See you tomorrow." I smiled at him and then started for home.

Just as I cleared the driveway, the heavens opened up and the rain fell in bucketfuls. Both

Dusty and I were drenched by the time we got home. I put her in her stall, untacked her, and rubbed her down.I gave her a little hay and water. Then ran to the house for ice to place on the spot on her front leg that felt hot when I touched it.

As I returned with the ice I turned on the radio and settled myself for a long night to watch over the mare. Rebel poked his head over the barn rail to see what all the commotion was about. Frank came into the barn with rain dripping from his slicker and said, "I saw the lights on and thought I would investigate what was going on." It was good to see Frank and though he would not be much help, he was a comfort. I took a deep breath and told him all that happened.

He just shook his head and said "Rotten bugger. Well, she always had that buck in her, but this time she hurt herself. It's not your fault. Looks like she is going back to being a field ornament for a while. You are a good-enough rider if you want to take on Rebel as Dusty heals."

My heart sank; it was not something I looked forward to. I had just gotten Dusty to the point where I wasn't embarrassed to ride with Brad at his fancy barn. Rebel was an unknown, and if he was anything like his name I was sure to be in for a challenge.

Opportunity Opens Her Door

The next day I was out on the back porch and I heard a knock at the front door. My sister Elaine went and answered it. Then she came and got me. "Nicole, it's for you. It's that boy. He's really cute," she said, raising her eyebrows and smiling.

"Oh, be quiet. That's all you can think about." I replied with embarrassment.

I then walked to the door with my head held high. As I opened the door, there stood Brad. He looked at me and asked, "How is it going? How is your bucking bronco doing?"

"Will you take a look at her?" I asked. "She hardly puts any weight on the leg and she has a hot spot with a good lump on it. I have been icing it and some of the heat is gone, but she is still limping," I explained.

"Sure, let's go," he replied.

We walked out to her pasture and Brad ran his hand down her leg. Then he walked her around. He looked at her in silence and finally said, "It's not bad, but the only thing is she is getting on in years and this may take some time to heal. I do have some news that might take some of the sting out of this."

"Oh, what's that?" I replied thinking to myself that no news could make this better. "Remember yesterday before you fell off how you were working on those figure eights on Dusty?"

"Of course. How could I forget? That ride was humiliating."

"Whatever! You took it like a pro," Brad said brushing off the remark.

"I practically am a pro—at falling off. She dumps me on the ground all the time," I said.

"No, you have come a long way and any horse can spook in those circumstances. Believe me you have become a pretty good rider under my tutelage," he teased. "Seriously, you learn fast and more than that you practice until you get it right. Not many people do that. Now don't get me wrong. You have a lot to learn, but you are not half bad. Now before your head gets too big let me tell you my news. Carol saw the whole thing. She was pretty impressed with your riding and even more impressed at how concerned you were about your bucking bronco. She wants to meet you! Do you know what this means?"

"Not really." I looked at him oddly.

"Nicole, she doesn't ask to meet just anybody. The last girl she thought was a good rider she asked to ride her top thoroughbred gelding. Then the girl went to nationals and now she is a high-class trainer with her own barn and clients. This meeting could open up a whole world for you! Carol likes to make things happen, and she enjoys seeing people succeed. She can't ride her own horses, so she asks people to ride them for her. Are you getting the picture?"

I looked at him with skepticism on my face letting his words seep into my brain.

Brad continued his enthusiasm building as he explained to me that Carol was aware of my love for horses and that the only horse that I had to ride was now lame. Then he asked me, "Do you remember that little bay mare you saw at the barn named Letty?"

That got my attention. I looked up at him as I was running my hand over Dusty's hot spot for the hundredth time, "Letty? Yeah, I remember her. What about her?" I said.

"Well, let's just say that she finished her training and Carol is looking for a rider for her. She asked me to talk to you about her."

I looked at him in disbelief, turning my head sideways waiting for the punchline.

"No, I am serious," he said raising his hand as if to shoo away my disbelief.

"What is the catch?" I asked.

"No catch," he said. She just asked me to ask you if you would be interested in riding Letty while your mare was healing. I said I would talk to you and see what your thoughts were. Well?" he said. "What are your thoughts?"

I stood there dumbfounded. Just minutes before I was looking at the prospect of a long winter with no horse to ride and feeling sorry for myself. Now here was Brad asking me if I wanted to ride my dream horse at a barn that I believed I would never be a part of.

I finally came out of my shock and said "My mother always says that when God shuts a door, he always opens a window. I guess this is my window, and I better take advantage of it. What do I need to do?" I asked, as I stroked Dusty's soft muzzle.

"Not much. Just come to the barn tomorrow afternoon and I will introduce you to Carol. From there you are on your own."

That night as I lay on my bed on the three-season porch with covers tucked up under my chin I breathed a prayer of help. "Please, don't let me blow this," I cried from my heart. I listed all the reasons why this couldn't work. My family didn't have the money. I didn't have the right kind of clothes and my mother would think it was foolish. My list went on until my heart was empty of all its fears. Then up from my heart floated a verse from Sunday school. "My God shall supply all of your needs according to His riches in Glory." My thoughts mulled that verse over and over in my head on that night as I looked at the stars from my window. I breathed a second prayer toward heaven and said, "I have some needs and some of your riches in glory would sure come in handy." A deep peace finally came over me as I drifted into sleep on that cool autumn night.

As soon as I jumped off the school bus I ran to the house and rushed through the few small chores that were expected of me. I did not want anything to get in my way of finally meeting Carol. I had not told anyone about what Brad said to me the day before about Letty. All day long I daydreamed about meeting Carol and riding Letty. My friends at school teased me and asked if I had a new boy-friend. I just shrugged it off. I knew that no one would understand all the excitement I had about horses, and this was so near and dear to me I didn't want them to scoff at my dream.

I called to my mother who was teaching an art class in our backroom that doubled as her art studio and our family room. "Mom," I yelled, "I am going to the equestrian center to meet Brad."

"I thought Dusty was hurt," she replied.

"I am going to ride my bike over there," I responded and held my breath, hoping she would not come up with a reason to delay my meeting.

"Did you do your chores?" she asked.

"All done," I said.

"Well, be careful around those animals. Do not be late for dinner and most of all do not come to the dinner table stinking like horses," she replied as she turned back to her art student.

"No problem," I said as I grabbed a cookie, running out the door toward my bike.

The day was beautiful and crisp. The leaves had fallen from the trees, and the world was getting ready to dress itself for winter. My mind was whirling with incomplete thoughts and adrenaline coursed through me as my legs pumped my bike pedals. A whole new world was about to open before me, and my mind could not quite comprehend what that would all entail.

Brad met me as I parked my bike. "I don't know where Carol is right now, but she should be around here somewhere. When she sees you she'll most likely introduce herself to you. I need to throw some hay to the horses in the north pasture so I won't be around for a couple minutes. Is that okay?" Brad said.

"Yeah, that's fine. Do you need any help?" I asked.

"No, I have the four wheeler loaded up with hay, and there is only room for me," he replied.

"Is it okay if I look around?" I asked.

"Go for it. I'll find you later," he said as he turned to feed the horses.

I felt a little awkward walking around the barn all by myself. I decided to find Letty. I wandered around until I found her stall. She wasn't in it. I started to look around, when I noticed a schedule on her stall that indicated that she was supposed to be in the east pasture at this time. So, I started to walk outside. I spotted Letty in the pasture with someone standing next to her petting her. I thought that it was one of the workers getting ready to take the horses in for the night. I hopped over the fence and started walking over to her.

"Hey, there!" I said when I came up to Letty and woman beside her. "I'm Nicole," I said, as I extended my hand towards the woman. "Do you need any help?"

"Hello," the woman said. She looked middle aged with wonderful red hair and smiling brown eyes. She stood about five feet, seven inches with an athletic build that exuded an energy and confidence that unnerved me a little, yet reeled me in. She gave me a friendly smile, shook my hand, and nodded her head at me. "Isn't she a cutie?" she asked, stroking the horse's dark neck.

"She's beautiful," I said. Letty started to nose at my pockets sniffing for treats. I laughed, "Why you little beggar!" After she inspected me and saw that I had no treats she put her head back down and began to eat. She stayed between the two of us, grazing in the cool, crisp, autumn air as we talked.

"She likes you," she stated.

"Oh, how do you know?" I asked.

"See how she just stays here between us." she said.

"Yeah," I said.

"Horses are herd animals and honest. Usually, when a stranger comes into their herd they move away from them. She is almost leaning into you. You must have a real feel for horses."

I laughed, "Oh, this one here knows me and knows that I am one of her biggest fans. My friend Brad works here, and any time I come here I look for her and tell her how wonderful she is and give her a treat. We are friends."

Carol

"I'm Carol Lennards," said the woman as she extended her hand once again. I shook it and was surprised at the friendliness and energy of the woman There was something about her that made me really comfortable. The uneasy feelings I had all day started to slip away.

I was not sure where I had gotten the idea of what Carol would be like, but I had somehow had made her into a cold, distant person who weighed everything you did with expectations that could never be met. I had visions of meeting her in the office with her sitting behind a desk with jewels on and a cold stare, inspecting me like some bug to see if I was worthy of her company. I never expect to meet Carol in the pasture with her horses dressed as a work hand. Here she was standing full of warmth and acceptance and an open heart toward me. Oh, I had a lot to learn about her. I was beginning to see why Brad thought so highly of her.

"Brad said you wanted to meet me." I said that to put a distance between the awkward shyness that was starting to creep over me. I had envisioned this meeting a million different ways, but this was not one of them.

"Yes," she laughed. "The display you put on was pretty impressive. You stuck on that mare like glue!" she teased.

"Oh gosh, she had not done anything like that for ages. I don't know what got into her." I started to give excuses for her behavior.

Carol put her hand on my arm and said, "I'm just teasing. Seriously, I have been watching you all summer. I have seen you take a grumpy old mare and turn her into a respectable saddle horse, though she is a smart one and does like to take advantage. You have done a wonderful job with her."

"I don't know if I could have done it without Brad. He has been great and gives me pointers all the time." I replied.

"Yes, the two of you have become quite the pair," she said with a twinkle in her eye. She continued, "Brad is one of my favorites, and he really knows his stuff. He is a natural and horsemanship has come easy to him. When he is around the horses are always more relaxed. I always have him hold the horses when the veterinarian and farrier come and we see a lot less trouble. Yes, there is something special about that boy. How is the mare doing?" she said changing the subject.

"Dusty is lame. There is a hotspot on her left front leg, and no matter how much I ice it, that lump will not go down. I was so looking forward to riding this winter," I said, dejected.

"Yes, I understand that feeling. I would give almost anything to be able to ride again. I was in a car accident and broke my neck. I am lucky to be walking. The doctor said no more riding. It is just not worth the risk. I am learning how to drive a buggy and can still do all the groundwork, but it is not the same as being on board and feeling the partnership that riding brings. Brad tells me that you are as crazy about horses as I am. He said you were the most persistent person he has ever met. He told me all about how you cleaned up the pasture, took on that cranky mare, and worked with her until she was safe to ride. He said you even cleaned up the barn so it was usable again. Yes, he has a high opinion of you," she said again with that twinkle in her eye.

"Well, that's nice to know," I said. "He is always telling me how I can do things better. What to do, how to do it, and when to do it. He is full of advice, and I guess I don't mind because I really did not know much about horses. He is right, though. I am a little crazy about them. I love just being in their company and a part of their world. Sometimes things can get pretty tense in our house, and I go to the barn to be with the horses because it is always so peaceful. Frank, our neighbor, owns the horses and the barn. He is great but does not know much about horses. We made a deal that I could ride if

I took care of them. They were his kid's horses. When they grew up and moved away he did not have the heart to sell them. I wanted to ride more than anything, so I took him up on his deal. Most of what I have learned was from books."

"Then one day I saw Brad riding in the woods and we became friends. He started giving me short riding lessons on our trail rides. He said he did not want to see me get killed. He is always saying things like that. He is such a good rider. I did not know that horses could move like that. So, I decided to listen to him and learn as much as I could. I call him 'Mr. Know it all'. I feel like I am always asking questions and worry that he thinks I'm just a little annoying kid."

"Oh, don't worry about Brad. I think you even surprise him. When you are not here he is only full of praise for you. He has even made me a fan," she laughed.

As we walked back toward the barn Carol said "I have a deal I would like to make with you."

When she said that my stomach started to get a flutter.

"What's that" I replied.

She started out by saying "My family did not have much money all through my childhood. Now that I'm more fortunate, I look for ways to share what I have with those who also have a great love for horses. I can see we share that love. Brad has told me that money might be an obstacle for you so, this is my deal: you can ride and show Letty this season. I'll pay for the trainer, care, and show expenses, but you must ride her. I bought her to be my buggy horse, but she has a little too much zip in her and needs a few seasons under her belt to make her a safe carriage horse. So, you would be doing both of us a favor. Is it something you would consider?" she asked.

"You must be joking! It's like a dream come true! Riding is not a problem! Oh my," I stuttered. "I can't believe this!"

"Wonderful! Let's contact your parents and work out all the details," she said.

That statement was the only thing that really worried me. I knew my dad would be alright with this, but my mom did not like horses. She thought they were dangerous and she did not like it that I spent so much time in the barn. She was always worrying and trying to talk me out of this "horse phase" that I was in.

"Oh God," I pleaded, "don't let her blow this."

Arrangements were made and Carol came over to our house the next evening. My mom and dad asked me what this was all about and I told them best I could. Mom was skeptical, but Dad thought it was a great opportunity. It was moments like this that I just loved my dad. All my mother would say is, "We'll see."

When Carol came over I made the introductions. My mom told me to wait in the kitchen while they talked in the family room. I paced back and forth, wondering what my fate would be. I heard Carol talking as they shut the door. A half hour went by when I heard them laughing. I thought, *That has to be good*. I hoped it was good. Another ten minutes crawled by.

"Please God let her agree, please," I whispered.

The door finally opened, and out they came. First my Dad came out, followed by my mother and Carol.

"Well?" I asked.

"Well, what?" replied my mother.

"Can I ride at Carol's barn?" I pleaded.

No one said anything. I could hear the clock ticking in the room. My heart began to sink. All their faces were blank. I could not tell what they were thinking.

My mother finally broke the silence with, "You cannot neglect your schoolwork, chores, and most of all you have to promise me you won't do anything foolish."

I looked at her and said, "Does that mean yes?"

She nodded her head, and I ran to her, hugging her and promising her the world. Everyone laughed, and I couldn't believe my good fortune. Under my breath I breathed a thank you toward heaven.

Letty

I jumped off the school bus the next day and raced toward the house to zip through my chores and grab a bite to eat. I did my homework on the bus, which became my habit throughout high school. My chores consisted of feeding my big cat Max and cleaning out his litter box. I also had to make sure the kitchen and entryway were tidy because my mother's art students walked through them to get to their lessons. It only took a few moments to put things in order. I had promised I would keep up with it and did not want to lose the privilege of going to the barn.

I met Brad and Carol at the barn where they showed me where they kept Letty's tack and brushes. They went over the schedule of where the horses were throughout the day. It was a small map with horses' names in each pasture that was kept in the feed room next to the telephone.

Brad explained, "You have to be careful what mix of horses you put together so that one does not get picked on. You have to introduce them slowly because a new horse can really get beaten up if not properly introduced. Always make sure you have her in with her buddies, or it could be bad for her."

"Letty is usually out in the pasture until dinnertime. We give them at least an hour after dinner before we ride them; it gives them time to eat their dinner, and they are happier about their work."

I walked out to her pasture and there she was. I just watched her graze for a while not wanting to rush the wonder of the moment. I eventually grabbed the carrot I had put in my pocket for her, offering it to her as I easily slipped the halter on her head and led her back to the barn.

Brushing and saddling Letty was so different than Dusty. She was so willing and not once did she pin her ears at me. Whoever trained her had been gentle and patient with her. As I touched her leg to clean her feet she gave me her foot without any objection. Her coat shined as I brushed her. She stood about fifteen hands, three inches with nice, straight legs, a sturdy muscled back, and almost perfect conformation. She was not a huge horse but a nice size for me. I whispered to her as I brushed her that we were going to be great friends and to please be patience with me as I learned how to handle her.

I was to meet Brad at the indoor arena. This made me a little nervous because I had never ridden in one. Everything seemed so foreign. I didn't know the unspoken rules and that made me uneasy. I finally followed a man with a large chestnut gelding into the arena and noticed before he opened the door he yelled, "*Door!*" I guessed he did that so people knew we were coming in and no one was caught by surprise. It was little things like that that I tucked away to ask Brad about later. I wanted to know all the proper etiquette that made this barn run. I dreaded the idea of sticking out.

"Well, are you going to get on that horse and ride her or just stand there?" Brad teased.

I was so happy to hear his voice. Everything was so new to me, and I wasn't sure what to do next.

"Hop on and I will give you a short lesson. Just walk her around this half of the arena a few times so that you get use to each other." He put a pole on the ground and then had me do figure eights over it at a walk, trot, and canter. This put me at ease because it was an exercise that we had done on Dusty. That was the only thing about her that was like Dusty. She was much more sensitive than Dusty. If I moved my head to the left, she would move to the left. If I leaned forward, she would move along faster at whatever gate we were in. If I sat up to ask for the canter, she was ready for it and just moved along. She loved to work, all at high speed if I would let her. Most of my first ride was just quieting me down so that I did not give her mixed signals. She was a challenge and pleasure to ride.

As I was taking her saddle and bridle off, Brad came to see how I was doing. He showed me how to use the wash stall which was a nice change from the cold hose I would use on Dusty.

"She is a good match for you. You will learn a lot from her. She is due to foal in early spring. Carol does not want her jumping anything more than cross rails. We can work on your equitation and dressage for the rest of the season." Brad said.

"That gives you the winter show season on her before the baby is due. Carol was also wondering if you would like to join the Pony Club here," Brad said.

"I have some of their books. I used to just pour over them when I was first learning to ride Dusty. I love those books. If the club is anything like the books, that sounds like something I would be interested in," I answered.

"Yea, Pony Club is big on rules, but you learn a lot. Some of the best riders I have seen were part of The Pony Club. They don't just teach about riding, they teach you horsemanship. They are an international voluntary youth organization for young people interested in riding and have been the starting point for a large majority of equestrian team members and Olympic medal winners. If you go through all the pony club levels you will be a master equestrian. You would know how to ride, teach, train, and run an equestrian center. It is really quite a program," Brad explained.

"It sounds great. How do I join?" I asked.

"Talk to Carol. She knows all about it. She is in the office, and I know she would love to hear about how your ride went," he replied.

As soon as I had Letty all put away, I went to see Carol. It was so much fun talking with her. She loved to hear all the details, both good and bad. This was the start to a wonderful relationship that continued throughout my life. We talked about the Pony Club, and she got me into the club that night with a phone call.

Pony Club had mounted meetings where everyone from the club would get together on their horses and work on their riding. We also had unmounted meetings where we worked on equestrian knowledge. I really enjoyed the club and the people in it, but always seemed to have trouble with one of the girls. On one of the first mounted clinics for Pony Club I came up to a group who were on their horses waiting for their turn to ride and heard them talking.

"Who's the new girl?" one of them asked.

"Rebecca, one of the best riders, replied "Oh, that's one of Carol's charity cases."

That stung, but also made me a little mad. I knew I had to get along with this group because Carol wanted me in the club. So, I swallowed my pride.

As I came into the group, I quipped, "Just call me Charity."

They all looked at me with surprise and then broke into laughter. From that day on I was known as Charity.

Most of the kids had been in the club for a while and knew how to ride pretty well. I was the new kid riding a horse I did not own. I did not mind; I just wanted to learn to ride. They could make as much fun of me as they wanted to. My focus was on learning and Letty was my dream horse. I was on cloud nine and they could not take that away from me.

We were all competitive, but the club taught us that we had to work as a team. In all of the competitions you were placed in teams and your success depended on the others. The more interdependent your team was the better success you had.

The show season was mediocre because I had no experience. I learned that losing wasn't bad and winning was great.

Dusty finally healed. I continued to take care of Franks barn and my old friend. I would hop up on her bareback and ride her around the pasture a couple of times a week. She seemed to enjoy the attention. Whenever she saw me heading toward the barn she would start toward me.

Frank's daughter Liz came and watched me ride Dusty one afternoon. She could not believe the difference in her. I patted her neck sharing the stories of how we had gotten to this point. She told me how Dusty had been her 4-H project and how much fun she had had on her as a kid. We both laughed about her naughty antics swapping stories one more outrageous than the next. Even with all her quirks she had taught us both so much and you could tell we had a soft spot in our hearts for her. We both agreed that with consistent riding she had become a nice saddle horse. Liz told me she had a daughter who was eleven years old and crazy about horses. She was wondering if I would work with her daughter and teach her how to ride Dusty. I was happy to share the responsibility of my old friend and agreed to teach her what I could.

That very next week Frank's granddaughter Lucy showed up at the barn and we started our lessons. I had learned so much from Brad and the Pony Club that putting a small lesson together was much easier than I thought it would be. I showed her how to catch Dusty from the pasture. We took a small carrot for her and she let us put her halter on her without much trouble. I shared with Lucy the first time I had tried to catch Dusty from the pasture, and we both had a good laugh. Next I showed her how to groom and saddle her from the cross ties. After that we found a nice large level area in the pasture and marked it off with some large boulders from the creek to make an arena. That was the beginning of lessons that went on for many years. Lucy was my first student and we shared that special love for horses that gave us an unbreakable bond of friendship.

Lucy spent most of her summer with her grandfather so she could ride Dusty. My old friend had found a new partner and I was glad for both of them.

My mom loved the Pony Club. She was all about safety and rules. She would even help me memorize all the items you needed to know to pass to each level. In the Club, you are rated to a standard that starts out at the lowest level which is D1 and moves up to the A level. I wanted to become an A rider and started to push myself hard toward that goal. Carol and Brad helped me and were my greatest advocates.

By the end of the season, Letty was no longer able to be ridden. The baby inside of her was starting to grow larger. The foal was due in April. So, over the winter I rode other horses that Carol wanted exercised. Brad continued to give me lessons and it was that winter that I learned to jump. It opened up a whole new world for me. Brad would have me do course work where I would jump a series of jumps in a certain pattern. I would get so focused on my form that I would mess up the order of the jumps. Brad was always telling me the order of the course. I am sure I tried his patience.

No matter which horse I was riding at the time none of them were as important as Letty. She held a special place in my heart. After I finished with the other horses, I would always get Letty and take her on long walks and let her graze while I brushed her. I would sit with her and dream about the baby she had hidden inside of her.

She was bred to a large chestnut horse named Higha Bob Leo who stood sixteen hands, three inches tall. He was a bold, athletic mover that could fly over a course without any effort. He was full of courage and would jump anything. His flat work was flawless, and he floated when he moved. He was grace in motion. Everyone's eyes would follow him no matter what he was doing. He was an up-and-coming national star on the eventing circuit. On his way home from a show one night a drunk driver hit the trailer he was in and they had to put him down. Letty was carrying the only foal he would ever have. So, this baby was going to be something special. I just knew it.

New Life

Carol wanted me to be there when the foal was born. On the night that Letty gave birth I received a call in the middle of the night from Carol. I had been anticipating this for the last couple of weeks. I had placed my clothing and shoes next to my bed, so I could slip into them without waking anyone. I left a note on the kitchen table and raced to get my bike.

My bike speedily sliced through the night over a country road I had traveled many times. The stars twinkled, singing silently in the night sky, and the whole world seemed like it was asleep. I whispered a prayer of safety for Letty and the foal. I got there as fast as I could. I dumped my bike next to the barn.

There was an unusual stillness to the barn. A tension like creation was holding its breath waiting for this birth. There was no sound and the only light was from the moon and stars shining through the windows. I could walk to Letty's stall blindfolded so the lack of light did not unnerve me. It was just this unusual stillness that made me nervous. The barn was normally so full of activity. As I headed toward Letty's stall, I noticed a soft light coming from it. I spotted Carol and Brad outside the stall watching. Everything was so quiet except for the groans coming from Letty. Carol reassured me in a whispered tone that everything was going smoothly. Within minutes the foal was born. I had never witnessed a birth before, so the miracle of it took me by surprise. First there was only one horse in the stall, and then suddenly, there were two. Each with their own life and distinct personality.

She was all wet and wobbly, dazed by the sudden change of environment. Letty immediately started to lick her down to get her circulation going.

The first thing I spotted was the white blaze on her forehead that was just like her sire's and one white sock on her back left leg.

"She going to be a bay," I said, with a grin on my face that just could not be stopped. "It's a girl."

"What do you think of her?" Carol asked in hushed tones.

"She is one of the most beautiful creatures I've ever seen." I smiled at her.

All at once I started to hear the other horses nickering. It was if they were singing to her. The sound grew louder and stronger and lasted for only a few moments but etched themselves on my heart for eternity. Goose bumps spread across my whole body as I sat and listened to their beautiful song for this new creature God had placed in this barn. The whole barn had filled with a chorus of greeting to the new foal.

"What is going on?" I said as I looked around.

"They are welcoming her into the world, but I have never heard them quite so adamant about it before. There must be something special about this one," Carol grinned looking at me. She continued, "I think it is one of the most fascinating threads of life God places in horses that connects them. Herds do this when a horse is born and when they die. It is really quite amazing how all the horses know when an event like this occurs. It gives me goosebumps every time this happens."

We walked into the stall, talking quietly to Letty and asking her permission to let us take a good look at her new baby. She seemed fine with us entering her stall and touching her baby. I took some nice clean towels and helped wipe her down, noticing the exceptional way her tiny body was put together.

Carol explained she would stay with the foal until it nursed for the first time. That's when she asked me, "This is a very nice filly, don't you think?"

"She is amazing," I said as I rubbed her small forehead.

"I'm glad you think that. Would you like to have this filly?" she said as she looked me straight in the eye. I just stared at her as if I had heard her wrong.

"Do you like your new filly?" She repeated again.

"You cannot mean it! You are kidding!" I stood not moving while the reality of what she said seeped into my brain. I looked from Carol to the foal, and then tears rolled down my cheeks as I hugged Carol. She put her arms around me and said, "I would have asked you before, but I wanted to make sure everything was going to be fine with the foal. She looks like she is going to be a beauty."

At that moment this beautiful filly decided to try to get to her feet for the first time. After a few attempts, she was on her feet checking out the world. She found her mother and nursed. She was beautiful, strong, healthy, and she was mine. Now all I had to do was talk my mom into letting this dream come true.

"Nicole, Carol, move in. I want to get a picture of this," Brad said motioning us together to get the shot. I put my arms around my new filly, and Carol stepped behind us. I looked down and held the foal in my arms. She looked up at me unafraid with her large, soft brown eyes.

I said goodbye to Carol and Brad as they went back to their warm beds. I just could not get myself to leave and I spent the rest of the night in the stall with the pair of them. I could not believe what had taken place. My dream of owning a horse had just come true. At least she was mine if I could get my parents on board with this, but that was going to be a challenge. I know my dad would go along with whatever my mom decided. I let my mind focus on all the possible objections my mother could have. Then I took each one, coming up with answers that would counteract any of them. As the stars and moon shined through the window that night, I asked the good Lord to help me put together a plan that would convince my mother that this was a good thing. I could make it work of course, with His help.

As the sun was rising I dragged myself away from the barn knowing that my family would be looking for me. I walked into the house to see my mother having her first cup of coffee and scanning the newspaper. My mother's eyes peaked above the paper, and she asked, "Did Letty have her baby?"

"Oh Mom, you would not believe how amazing this whole night was. Letty's foal is absolutely the most wonderful thing I have ever seen. She is a cute little bay with a blaze and one white sock just like her dad. It only took her a few minutes to stand and eat. And the most wonderful thing happened when she was born. All the horses in the barn welcomed her to the world with a beautiful nickering that sounded like a song that gave me goosebumps. I will never forget it if I live to be a million years old. Carol said they always do that, but not as enthusiastically as they did for this one. She thinks that is because there must be something special about her. She also said she was mine if you would agree."

With that last statement she put the paper down on her lap and raised her eyes toward heaven and her mouth dropped open and nothing came out she just stared at me. I was hoping that was good.

"Say that last part again," she said in disbelief.

I started out with the speech that I had put together while I had shared those first few moments of my horse's life. "Well, I know you probably can't believe anyone could be as generous as Carol, and I am having a hard time believing it myself. I know a horse is a huge responsibility, and there would be costs involved, but I have figured out how I can cover that. Also, for the first six months, the baby will be with her mother, and Carol said there would not be any cost. So, for six months I can start saving and get ahead to pay for her bills. Brad said he would help me train her and you know I will stay in the Pony Club. With all their good safety rules it will be fine." I said trying to put any objections to rest before she could start.

"What do you think?" I asked.

"Well, I can see you have put a lot of thought into this, but I would like to talk it over with your father before you take on such an extravagant gift," she said. "I know you are crazy about horses, and I know you will take good care of her, but to be honest the unknown costs have me worried," she answered.

I started in again, "I promise that if she becomes a burden, we can sell her. I have a deep feeling she is going to be exceptional. If she is as fine as I think she will be, we can get all of our money back. I can get a job after school to pay for her. They are always looking for people at the convenience store. I know if you say yes, Dad will go for it. So, what do you say? Please let me try and do this."

She sat there staring at me for the longest time, and then all at once she said, 'Have you picked out a name for her? You know a name is a very important thing."

I named the filly Ella, and it fit her perfectly. She had the best attributes of both of the mare and stallion.

The Mares Pasture

That spring three foals were born and they were kept in a special pasture with their mothers. Ella was the last of the new ones to be born. She spent the first couple of days in her over-sized birthing stall but the time to go out into the world had come. I was nervous and trying not to show it. I came extra early to the barn to walk the pasture one more time to make sure there was not something she could get hurt on. I had heard some horrible stories about young ones getting caught up in fencing and I was going to make sure that did not happen to Ella.

Brad came up behind me as I was staring into Letty's stall and he said, "Don't worry so much; she will be fine. Letty is a good momma and won't let anything bad happen to her."

I exhaled, "Are you sure? I just want this to go smoothly. Tell me the plan one more time."

"Okay now this is how it will go. After Letty is done with her breakfast we will put her halter on her and lead her to the pasture. You be the one to lead her because she is used to you and trusts you. I will go behind at a respectable distance to make sure Ella doesn't try to go back to the stall. She will be nervous and should stay close to Letty. We will make sure all the stall doors are closed so they act like a shoot to the open pasture that is attached to the end of the barn. We only have one corner to turn to get there. Now let's do this! Letty is done with her breakfast."

The moment had come and we were going to introduce Ella to the outside world. I went into the stall and put the halter on Letty. I took her in a large circle toward the open stall door. Letty called to her baby to come to her side. Letty kept nickering at her to keep her close as we headed to the pasture. Everything seemed to be going just fine until we came to the corner. I had taken my eye off of Ella as we turned the corner. Just at that moment the old tom cat Max, decided to investigate what was happening. Ella stopped in her tracks at the sight of that old tom cat. She put her nose down to investigate Max losing sight of her mother. Letty let out a sharp winnie calling Ella back to her side. Ella had lost sight of her mother and panicked. She started to whinny to her mother and Letty gave a sharp pull on the lead line answering her back. I heard the scurry of little hooves on isle and Brad's quiet low voice encouraging her to move forward. Just when I thought this whole episode was going to fall apart, I saw Brad with Ella in his arms showing her her mother. He set her down and Ella stayed like glue to her mother's side not letting any daylight show between them as we walked to the pasture.

Once we made it outside I walked Letty around the pasture. I made sure she and Ella got a good look at the fenceline. The pasture was nice and large with the new grass of spring just starting to pop up. Off to the left of the pasture stood a large old willow that would give plenty of shade for those hot summer days that lay ahead.

"Nicole, you have to let Letty off her lead line. She will take care of Ella. Now give them some space. We will stay behind the fence and watch for a while in case anything happens. Then we will bring in the other mothers and their foals to meet them. We do this all the time. Believe me, she will be Okay."

"That little incident in the isle of the barn had unnerved me more than I thought," I laughed.

"The first time out of the stall to the pasture can be tricky. They get the routine down in a couple of days. We will be careful with her until she knows her way around. Most babies stick close to their momma, but this one is curious and a little independent and that could get her into trouble. Chief will put her in her place and teach her to keep out of trouble."

"Who is Chief?" I asked.

"Chief is an old gelding the size of a small house. He was a roping horse in his day. Carol bought him as a trail horse for her husband to ride. He loves the foals and babysits for the mares during the day. He let us know that he thought that the foal pasture was where he belonged. He would stand across from the mare and foal pasture and just stare day after day and would nicker at the babies. Carol put him in the pasture one day just to see what would happen. The mares let him know his place real fast but, within hours that big horse was babysitting for those mares. He makes sure the foals behave themselves. If their play gets too rough he steps in and straightens out the situation before anyone gets hurt. If a foal lays down to sleep he stands over them keeping vigil. The mares get to graze and the whole herd is just so much more relaxed with him overseeing them all."

" I can't wait to meet this big fellow. How do we introduce the other horses?" I asked as I slipped off Letty's halter.

"We introduced the other mares and foals one at a time until they feel comfortable with each other." Brad reassured me.

Letty was a great mom. She let the other horses know without a shadow of a doubt that if they messed with her baby they would pay. Finally, we brought Chief out to meet Ella. Letty marched over to him, squared off with her ears pinned, teeth bared, stomping her feet and squealing, letting him know that this was her baby. Chief just stood there giving the pair of them a respectful distance. It was as if he was saying, "Don't worry momma I am only here to help." He had a gentle old soul and believed his job in this life was to watch over those babies, and making the mommas comfortable was part of the job.

After everyone found their place in the herd, the foals began to play with each other. They would play chase and rear up on their hind legs just enjoying life. If one of them ever got too far from the herd, Chief was always there to make them come back with a gentle nip. The mares got to depend on his help with those rambunctious babies that seemed to have a never ending amount of energy and curiosity. Ella was especially full of curiosity and loved to run. She would always instigate races with the other foals running in large circles around the mares as they grazed. Chief was always there watching, and if he thought Ella's circles were getting too far away from the herd he would let her know.

One day, a coyote decided to take a shortcut through the mare's pasture. I was getting a horse from the far pasture for my weekly riding lesson when I noticed him. He was a rangy old boy that was about to be taught a lesson that would almost take his life.

The foals were playing and racing around which must have pricked his interest, and he went to investigate. I saw him slink down and begin to move slowly across the ground. I screamed for help running toward the mare's pasture. The scene before me was terrifying me. Somehow he had gotten Ella separated from the herd and had her cornered. I heard her squeal and stomp her feet trying to get out of the corner. She would move one way and he would anticipate the movement driving her farther away from the herd. I knew I would never have enough time to get to her before something would happen. Then like a flash, I saw Chief on top of that old coyote. He grabbed the coyote by the scruff of the neck with his teeth and violently shook it back and forth. He then threw him to the ground and came galloping at him with death in his eyes. At the last moment that coyote ducked under the fence running for cover never to be seen again. By the time I got to the pasture Ella was standing next to her mother nursing for comfort. I was shaking as I ran my hands over her to make sure nothing had happened. Once I was convinced she had no injuries I turned to look over the pasture to make sure everything was in order. Chief stood looking in the direction of where that coyote had run, his body tense and alert. I walked toward him whispering my thanks to him. When I reached him I gave that tough old horse with so much heart a huge hug and the treat I kept in my pocket. His body stayed alert as he accepted the hug and treat that he knew was his reward.

That night I gave him a couple extra handfuls of grain. I stood and talked with him as he ate his dinner expressing my thanks for all that he did for the mares and foals; especially for my naughty little Ella.

After the coyote incident Ella seemed to hang out with Chief more and more. She would graze with him nose to nose. I would often find her standing next to him watching over the herd. Ella had found a new hero and if she could pick up his loyalty and bravery that would be fine with me. You can do as much training as you like to make a horse stronger and to improve its way of going, but it is the heart and its generosity that will separate the good horses from the top ones. Chief was all heart and if he could give some of that to my Ella I would always be grateful.

It was now time to halter train Ella. I had read many different ways of halter training. Natural horsemanship seemed the best way to go and it was something Brad and I agreed on. I had spent a couple hours each day running my hands and a soft brush over Ella's small body. Introducing a halter was not hard. Brad had halter trained many foals and was happy to teach me to train her.

"Let's get that filly of yours halter trained. We have a couple of hours before the horses come in for the night and for once all the chores are done. What are you waiting for? Let's go!" Brad urged.

We took them into the arena and led Letty around, letting Ella follow her momma. She wanted to stop at every corner and investigate everything, but Letty kept calling her to her side and she would reluctantly obey. We next took the pair of them to the middle of the arena where we made Letty stand still. Ella stood next to her but all her attention was on me as I ran my hands and the small halter over her body. Brad stood next to Letty with an eye on me. He started giving me instructions in a calm soft voice.

"Keep talking to her softly, and let her sniff the halter; then rub it up and down her neck and back, letting her know it won't hurt her. Don't rush, take your time. Once she ignores it just slip it over her nose until that becomes easy. After that, slip it over her head until that becomes easy. Last of all you want to tie it off and let her feel the weight of it. That's it. You got it. Take your time, no rush," Brad encouraged.

As I executed each instruction my complete attention was on what Brad was saying and the reaction I was getting from Ella. Little did I know that a small crowd had gathered to watch this training session. When I got to the point where I could tie off the halter the crowd started to clap.

Ella had never heard anyone clap and it startled her. She went from totally calm to a startled filly that was about to take flight. I tried to calm her with a soft voice making a grab for the halter to remove it, which only made matters worse. Ella jumped straight up in the air on all fours banging into me shaking her head. She kept shaking her beautiful little head and then decided to do a few laps around the arena, delighting the crowd and terrifying me. Letty called sharply to her and she came to her side. She started to nurse which comforted her and allowed me to remove the halter without any damage.

I swear that Ella loved the attention. She trotted out of the arena next to her mother with her head and tail held high as if saying, look at me I am special, as she passed the crowd. From that day forward she alway played to the crowd. The larger the crowd the more effort she put into her work. Yes, my Ella liked herself plenty and wanted the world to be aware of that fact.

The next six months passed by quickly and it was time to wean Ella from her momma. I was not looking forward to this day.

Frank suggested that I bring Ella to his small farm until she was ready to be trained. I talked it over with Carol and Brad and they both thought that would be a good idea.

Frank's farm was less than a mile away. The best way to move Ella to Frank's was to trailer her. I had to teach her about the trailer without her getting upset and hurting herself.

Chief had one last lesson to teach Ella. He was going to teach her how to ride in a trailer quietly. I took both Chief and Ella to the trailer the week before it was time for her to leave. I fed their dinners to them from the back of the trailer with the door open for two days. Then, I had Brad load up Chief and followed behind with Ella. As long as Chief was calm so was my six-month-old Ella. Their dinner was waiting for them as I loaded them. I closed the door behind them and let them eat their dinner. Ella leaned into the escape door but Chief stayed calm and this settled her.

The day arrived for Ella to leave the Equestrian Center and all that she knew. She was about to start a new life at Frank's. I had gone over the pastures and barn one last time to make them safe for her. I bedded down her stall and placed a small bucket of fresh water and hay for her. Next, I put Dusty in the stall next to hers with plenty of hay. She dove her head into it and started to eat. As she ate I gave her a lecture telling her all about Ella. I stressed that she had to be extra patient with her and teach her all about being a horse for the next couple of years. Rebel stuck his head over the gate, and I gave him a lecture also as I fed him a flake of fresh hay that he did not need.

Brad and Carol helped me load up Ella reassuring me that this was a good idea. Brad loaded Chief and, just as we had practiced, Ella followed him into the trailer where their treat awaited them. It took less than fifteen minutes to get to Frank's farm. We unloaded Chief first and Ella followed right behind. She looked around wondering where she was, but with steady Chief at her side she stayed calm. It was time to take Chief back home. It was as if that old horse knew this was the last time he was to see Ella. He put his large head over her withers gently nuzzling her and nickering his good bye.

I led Ella into her new stall and she looked around. Dusty popped her head up to see who the new horse next to her was but soon lost interest and started to eat. Rebel popped his head over the gate to see what all the commotion was. It was the first time I had ever heard him nicker. Ella pricked her ears and took a good look at him.

All of a sudden Ella realized that Chief wasn't there anymore and began to call for him. She called most of the night for her mother, friends, and the home she knew. I stayed with her late into the night but, finally went to bed knowing that she would not hurt herself.

The next morning I raced down to the barn to find Ella laying down in her stall sleeping. Rebel had kept his vigil at the gate all night. She had quit calling but she was nervous and jumpy. I fed her her breakfast and she ate, which was a good sign. I put her halter and lead rope on and walked the pasture showing her the boundaries. She had never seen a creek before and wanted nothing to do with it. I didn't push the issue knowing she could get used to it over time on her own.

It was time for her to meet the other horses. I had put Rebel in the barn along with Dusty and would introduce them one at a time. I unhooked her lead and she followed me to the barn. I let Dusty out first to meet her. She trotted up to her, gave her a good sniff, and finally squealed at her. Then she turned her back and promptly dropped her head to eat, ignoring her.

Rebel was next. I was not sure how he would be with her. Ella was a young horse but Chief had taught her a lot. She somehow won Rebel's heart. That is how it went from that day until she left. I would find Rebel grooming her and watching over her as she slept. He even played with her, teaching her all about the water in the creek that ran through the pasture. I would find them standing in the creek splashing on hot days and on cold winter days I would watch her fly over the creek just for the joy of it as Rebel forged through it. Rebel had found a job and it was watching over Ella.

Education For The Two-Year-Old

The next couple of years flew by. Ella was growing into a beauty. She was built like her father with his markings and her mother's coloring.

Brad stopped by the barn one day to help me teach Ella how to long line. After the lesson he suggested that we take Ella to a quiet local school show. He thought that it would be good step in her education.

"What class would I take her in? She's not even saddle trained?" I asked. "You could show her in hand. She is a beauty with nice conformation. She might do well. I would not go with any expectations of ribboning, but it will give her a chance to to learn to behave herself in spite of all the distractions that a show brings. I find if I have a goal with a horse I am more focused,the training moves along faster, and it will be easier to saddle train her when she is three." "What do I need to do to get her ready?" I asked.

"In preparation for the show ring she must learn to walk and trot out confidently and to stand square.

This in itself is a significant lesson because she must leave the other horses and trot away from them calmly and willingly without a backward glance and not a thought of being unruly. We will also need to pull and braid her mane. It's always nice to oil her hooves for the show ring also."

"Are there any classes Lucy could take Dusty in?, I asked.

"I am sure there must be some beginner classes."

"I was thinking if Dusty was there this would help to keep Ella calm and would be fun for Lucy. I don't have a way to get them to the show," I responded.

"That's not a problem. Carol said we could use her trailer. In fact it was her idea to get Ella to the show. She will probably drive the trailer too. She really loves this stuff. The show is in two weeks so that should be enough time to get you ready."

Brad was right. With the show in front of me my focus was sharp. I taught Ella to respond readily to my voice commands. Teaching her how to stand square and quiet was a challenge though. My young horse's attention span was short, and getting her attention for 60 straight seconds was a challenge. Getting her to move was easy. Having her stand still was a whole different world.

I would have her trot out next to me willingly and at my voice command halt and square up. Then she would lose her attention to a butterfly, or wind, or car passing the barn, or an ant crawling in the grass, or almost anything that would make it so she could not stand still. Ella was easy to train as long as she was moving, but someone forgot to tell her standing still was also part of the job description. Each day she stood just a little longer, but I had no illusions that at a horse show for the first time she would not be distracted.

Lucy was excited to take Dusty to the show. We picked out a few classes that we were sure Dusty was able to do. We had fun going through my old show clothes and found enough things that fit so she would be presentable.

Over the next couple of days we put a list together of all the items we would need for the show. We were missing a few items like traveling boots, hay nets, hooks for water pails and oil for the horse's hooves.

"What is the list for?" Frank said as he came into the small tack room Lucy and I were in.

"This is the list of items we need for the show. On the left side of the paper are the items we have and on the right side of the paper is a list of the things we don't have," Lucy said, looking up at her Grandfather.

Frank scooped up the paper eyeing the items and asked, "are you finished making the list? I am heading into town and would be happy to pick these items up for you. But, to be honest I'm not sure what all these items are or the best place to find them."

Lucy jumped up grabbing her grandfather's arm saying, "I can show you. I know the best place to go. Is that okay with you Nicole?"

"No problem, we are finished here. Tomorrow Brad said he would come over and do a run through with us on what to expect at the show. He said he would be over late afternoon and wanted you saddled and ready to go because he only has a short amount of time before he needs to head back and feed horses for the night. I thought we could do a sleepover, clean our tack and watch a movie. We need to get up extra early and have the horses ready when Brad and Carol swing over to pick us up. How does that sound to you."

"I don't know if I will be able to sleep. I'm so excited," replied Lucy.

"It's your first show. You are allowed to have a few jitters," I laughed. The classes we picked out for you and Dusty are a perfect fit for both of you. We are going to this show to get you some experience and to have some fun. There is no pressure. Now take your grandpa shopping and show him the best place to get horse equipment. You might want to think about show colors too."

"What are your colors Nicole?" Lucy asked.

"My colors are red and black to honor Ella's sire. They were his cross country colors. Also, I really like that combination. What are you favorite colors?"

Lucy looked around the room saying that she liked most colors. "Do I have to just pick two? Couldn't I have a rainbow of colors?"

I raised my eyes just picturing Dusty in a rainbow dust sheet with pink and lime green ribbons.

"These are the colors you will have for a long time so why don't you just start with two colors for now and you can always add on later if you want. Here, take a look at the catalog and see some of the combinations they have put together,"I handed the catalog to Lucy and turned my attention to Frank.

"That's awful nice of you to get all of this for us. Are you coming to the show?" I asked.

"I would not miss it for the world. It is the only thing Lucy has been talking about since you asked her if she wanted to show Dusty. She comes every day and practices. She makes me come and watch her ride, all the while asking me questions about her riding form. I wouldn't know good form one way or the other. The only thing I see is my granddaughter having the time of her life on a horse that I had given up just to be a pasture ornament. I have you to thank for that. She looks nice and secure up there and that gives me great pleasure. Thanks Nicole,"Frank said giving me a big smile.

I reached out and touched Frank's arm. I looked him in the eye and said, "It is me who should be thanking you. If you would not have given me the chance, I would still just be reading about horses. You got me started and I will always be grateful."

At that moment Lucy's head came up from the catalog and with a triumphant voice saying "I did it, I chose my colors."

"Well.....?" both Frank and I said at the same time.

"I chose hunter green and navy. Dusty will look great in those colors" she said as she handed back the catalog to me. She then grabbed her grand-father's arm and pulled him to the door toward the truck.

"I will be here extra early tomorrow and we can go through all the supplies." she said waving as she jumped into the truck with her grandfather.

I put everything in the tack room away and headed outside to watch the horses for a while. Ella picked her head up and noticed me at the fence. I called to her and she came from the bottom of the pasture jumping the creek without breaking stride. After her landing she picked up speed. It seemed like she was coming too fast and I began to wonder if she would jump the fence I was standing at. It would be an easy thing to do for her. Horses don't jump out of their pasture, but I was beginning to wonder if she would. At the last moment she put on the brakes posing with her head held high waiting for her treat. I gave the treat to her and patted her beautiful neck telling her to pose like this for the judge. It was as if she disliked my suggestion and suddenly spun galloping back to her friends. How was I ever going to get her to stand still for a judge to get a good look at her.

I didn't really care how we did at the show. I just wanted to get her off the farm and introduce her to the outside world in a safe environment. The words I had spoken to Lucy earlier came back to me. *We are doing this for the experience and for the fun of it. This is Good advice for myself I thought*.

I looked once more at the grazing animals. Ella was trying to get Rebel and Dusty to play with her. When she realized that they would not join her, she reared up, jumped forward, galloping a few laps around them just like she did as a foal before she settled down to graze with them. Standing still came in very small doses for her. It was if she was saying there is life out here so let's get to it. I had only one more year to wait before I could ride her and I was counting the days.

Brad came the next day as he promised. He went over with Lucy everything she could expect at the show bolstering her confidence. He was so patience with her answering her every question. Lucy had lots of questions and after he answered one she would say, "Yes, that was what Nicole said." It was like she was quizzing him making sure he would answer correctly.

Next it was my turn to run through the few thing I was expected to do at the show. Brad stood in the small arena at the bottom of the pasture waiting like a judge for me to trot up to him, square up Ella, and stand still while he walked around her giving her a good look over. She trotted off beautifully and squared up nicely, but when Brad moved to give her a look over she would begin to dance trying to see what he was up to. I teased Brad that he must look sneaky. She did not want to take her eye off of him. We finally got her to stand still when she realized Brad only wanted to walk around her.

Brad gave me some encouraging words saying,"She should be okay if the judge doesn't take too long to look at her. Two-year-olds can be unpredictable and this is her first time away from home since she was weaned. You can't really tell how she will be until we get there. She looks great. You have done a nice job with both horses. Let's get to the show nice and early so the horses have time to settle in before they go into the show ring."

After Brad left Lucy and I gave the horses a bath putting extra bedding in the stalls so they would stay clean. We gathered up our tack to give it a good cleaning getting ready for the next day.

The day of the show Lucy and I jumped out of bed as the sun was coming up. Frank met us at the barn with a small breakfast as we were braiding our horses and getting them ready to ride in the trailer.

Brad and Carol showed up just as we were putting the finishing touches on our horses. They helped load up all of our equipment checking each piece off the list Lucy and I had put together.

"It was amazing how many things we needed to take for such a small show," I said.

Carol replied, "Small show, big show, doesn't seem to matter. You need the same items. How does Dusty trailer?"

"I'm not sure. I know that she was taken to the fair as a 4-H project a couple of times so she must have been trailered for that. I guess we are about to find out."

Dusty gave the trailer a good look over but once she knew there was a treat waiting for her she loaded right up. Ella followed Dusty in and we were on our way.

The show was less than an hour away and we were some of the first people to get to the grounds. We unloaded the horses without any problems. Ella was looking around but stayed calm. Dusty was pretty unflappable and did not seem nervous about anything. She was going to be a good role model for Ella. I was so glad that we had brought her to keep Ella company. Lucy and I walked the grounds letting the horses get a good look at their new surroundings.

We had stalls for the horses in the small barn near the show ring. I had Lucy saddle up Dusty so we could pop over a few jumps in the show ring before they closed it for the start of the show. I took Ella with us making her stand still next to me as I schooled Lucy.

Once Brad saw that the horses were doing well he left us to sign both Lucy and me up for our classes. My classes were the first two of the show with Lucy's classes following a short time afterward. After Brad returned with the itinerary Carol and I put a few finishing touches on Ella. There was not one speck of dust on her coat that shined like a new penny when we were done.

I looked up from my work and noticed my family standing next to Frank. I was so surprised. I didn't think they would come. We had talked about it and I had said that Ella was only in two classes early in the morning and I was not expecting much from her at her first show. We had left it at that.

They walked towards me all talking at once, excited to be there. It was fun to see them. My dad leaned on the stall door with a grin on his face. Grandma was right next to him asking if she could pet Ella. I noticed my mother and sister were a couple of paces back but looked happy for me. This was one of the few times they had ever come to watch me with the horses. All at once I wanted to do well for my family. I wanted to show Ella off for them. Maybe they didn't share my passion for horses but they were there to support me.

It was time for me to get to the show ring. Brad and Lucy led the way with Dusty. Brad had thought if he kept Dusty near the ring that would help keep Ella calm. I was the last to enter the ring. There were twelve horses in my class. They all stood there perfectly still in line at the far end of the ring. The judge was at the other end of the ring waiting for the horses to come one at a time toward him at a trot so he could inspect them. I was the last to be inspected. I circled Ella a couple of times to keep her busy as we waited our turn. The horse next to me kept pinning his ears at Ella and fidgeting. I kept as much distance between them as I could. When my turn finally came I asked Ella to trot next to me away from the other horses. We started down toward the judge at a straight brisk trot. She stopped before the judge squaring up perfectly and I swear she was posing. The judged tipped his hat at me then started to inspect Ella. Just as he was coming around her back haunches someone decided to start a tractor that backfired. Ella jumped forward spinning around me a couple of times then stopped perfectly square posing once again. I could not help but laugh. There was no ribbon for that class but we had made it through and I had learned a lot.

For my second class I made sure to be one of the first ones to enter and stayed far away from that sour gelding from my first class. We were first to be inspected and this time I noticed the judge made a much larger circle around us. We got a ribbon in that class. Now it was time to turn my attention to Lucy and Dusty.

Thanks to Carol and Brad, Dusty was saddled and ready to go. My plan was to have Lucy do a few transitions from walk, trot to canter and then pop over a few little fences before she was to go into the show ring. Brad took Ella from me and started off toward the barn to put her in her stall. All at once Dusty started to whinny and she wouldn't stop. It was so unexpected, so unlike her. Poor Lucy was having a time of it. Dusty was only half listening to her and we just could not get her attention back. I sent my sister to tell Brad to bring Ella back. He had heard the winning but never thought it would be Dusty putting up such a fuss. As soon as Dusty could see Ella she got back to work.

"I thought we were bring Dusty to babysit Ella not the other way around," He said laughing.

"You can never tell what these horses are going to do. I'm just happy Dusty got back to work," I replied.

We kept Ella off to the side out of the way, but close enough so Dusty knew she was there. Dusty marched into the ring doing her course work like she had been doing it all her life. She took Lucy over her fences in a relaxed smooth rhythm. Lucy was thrilled. They ribboned in all of her classes which put a smile on everyone's face.

Frank and Carol came up to us as we were untacking Dusty and Frank Said "Not to bad for a pasture ornament."

I laughed and retold the story about the first time I had tried to jump a log in the Sister's Woods and how Dusty had reacted dumping me off. Lucy had never heard the story and made me tell it over and over again. We all had a good laugh and decided to round up our group and go for ice cream to celebrate the day.

Waiting to Grow Up

As I was waiting for Ella to grow up I continued to ride Letty at the Equestrian Center. Letty had become a good little jumper and enjoyed cross country. We entered many lower level events and my love of the sport grew with each event. She was a great partner that helped to put a nice solid foundation on my riding. Over the last three years she had settled down and was much steadier. She had matured just as Carol had predicted.

I really enjoyed Pony Club. I especially valued the emphasis our Club put on advancing your horse knowledge as much as your riding skills. I made many good friends, but I always seemed to have trouble with Rebecca. No matter what I did she always had a critical word for me or a nasty remark. I had let her remarks get to me and had started to to fire back every time she was critical of me whether I deserved the criticism or not. Problem was, Pony Club horse trials are a team sport and we were always put on teams together. So, I needed to put up with her or not be on the team. I was complaining about this to Brad one day when he stopped me in mid sentence.

"Can I give you a word of advice.?" he asked.

"Sure," I replied.I didn't like the look in his eye and I was sure he was about to give me a lecture.

"You like Pony Club. Rebecca is a part of it and is not going away. It looks to me as if you have two choices. You can either keep fighting and take all the fun out of something you love or you can take the high road and start treating her like you want to be treated. That is all I have to say, but I don't want to hear any more of your complaints about her."

He then gave me a hard look making his point. Without another word he walked away not waiting for a reply.

I did a lot of reflecting on what Brad said throughout the day feeling a little sorry for myself. I hadn't realized how negative I had become. The more I thought about it I could see that he was right. I was tying myself up in knots over Rebecca and becoming sour in the meantime. It was not good for our team to have this undercurrent of anger running through it. I am sure it made the others anxious. We were all competitive, and pulling together as a team would improve our chances of doing well. That night as I was drifting off to sleep I asked the Lord for his help and a plan that I could live with to overcome this situation.

I was able to put my plan to work that weekend. Our club was part of the regional horse trials of area IV. As we were setting up our stalls Rebecca came in late, breezing past me with a snide remark. Normally, I would have had a snide remark in return but today was a new day. Instead, I asked if she needed help unloading her equipment. She stopped in her tracks looked at me strangely like she wasn't sure she heard me right. I almost laughed out loud. *Taking the high road might actually be fun,* I thought.

Every time she was short with me or had a snide remark I returned it with a kind word or deed. No matter what she did, I did not let it get under my skin. It didn't make us best friends but by the end of that weekend we had a ceasefire. Our whole team benefited. The tension was out of the air. We were all more relaxed and performed much better than we ever had. Taking the high road had its benefits and produced great results too. I could turn my focus back on what I loved and that was learning as much as I could about horses.

"How did the weekend go?" Brad asked.

"I took your advice and I am happy to say that it worked wonders. I wish you could have seen Rebecca's face the first time I returned one of her snide remarks with kindness. She actually stopped in her tracks with her mouth open waiting for the punchline. All weekend long she kept trying to get under my skin, but she just couldn't. It was so much fun! There were a few times I wanted to let go with a zinger but held back and either ignored the slight or would turn it around on her. I think she finally realized how shallow she looked and kept her remarks to a minimum. I can't remember the team ever doing so well. It was wonderful."

"I am so glad for both of you," Brad said.

"I had no idea how much tension we had created until I stepped back and saw it from another point of view. I am sorry to say we had gotten into a pretty bad pattern. I'm glad you said something that helped to make it stop."

"I'm just glad to hear it has stopped. How did Letty do?" Brad said.

"She was great. The only trouble we had was at a ditch. She wanted to take a peek at it before she jumped over it. I had to re approach but she sailed over it without any trouble the second time. When we go cross country schooling I'd like to work on those. Most of the time they are not a big deal to her, but every once in awhile she decides there might be a boogie man in there. When I know there is one coming up I start anticipating the jump which makes matters worse."

"How did the Dressage go?" Brad asked.

"Not bad but I need to work on it. We had some nice moments with a few rough spots. I just need to learn to be more consistent with her. She makes up for it in her jumping. She loves to run cross country."

"Who loves to run cross country and jump?" Brad teased.

"Okay I love to jump and promise I will work on my dressage. But, she really does like cross country if we keep the ditches to a minimum," I laughed.

"How is Ella doing? Next week I am going to have some time. Do you want to train that horse of yours?"

That was music to my ears! Ella was turning three and the time had finally come. I was going to actually ride my fairy tail horse.

Under Saddle

*S*pring, with it's fresh face had finally arrived. It whispered of coming promises to be birthed. The creek was running strong, the new grass coming up in the pasture was lush, and the trees were starting to bud. Ella's third birthday was finally here! The time had come for Ella to have her first rider and it would be me! I had been dreaming of this since the day she was born.

Brad and I had done a lot of ground work over the winter teaching Ella to long line with all her tack on. She got used to her saddle and bridle and was attentive to voice commands. But no one had ever actually been in a saddle on her back.

As the day came closer for my first ride Carol's words echoed in my head; "*the way a horse is ridden and managed at the age of three as they are trained to saddle can influence the rest of their life. It is the most important stage of their career. This is when the foundation of trust, confidence and respect between the horse and their rider is established.*" I wanted this to be a good experience for both Ella and me and was determined to put in place the best possible experience for her that I could.

Carol came with Brad the first day we were to ride Ella. She had volunteered to help saying, "You never know what you might encounter on the first day of saddle training."

I was really grateful she had come. She was a natural with horses and had started many horses with great success. All of her experience training young horses was going to be needed that day.

I went and caught Ella. We took her into the barn and saddled her up as we had done all winter. Carol had us put a neck strap on her so that I could grab it if Ella lost her balance. I did not want to pull on the reins and catch her in the mouth.

Rebel stood at the barn door watching everything we were doing. He acted like an overprotective parent. As we led Ella toward the arena he followed close behind and tried to enter the arena with Ella. We had to shoo him away but he took up his vigil alongside the fence watching everything we were doing.

I walked up to him patting him on the neck telling him she would be just fine. He seemed to relax a little but did not leave his post at the fence.

Dusty kept a respectful distance and grazed pretending not to be interested in what we were doing. She was snatching at the grass in a nervous way that gave away her secret that she really did care.

The plan was to have Carol hold Ella. Brad would then give me a leg up. I would then lean over Ella's back letting her feel my weight on her back as we walked her around. Then once we were sure she was alright with that, I would sit up on her. If that went smoothly we would then lunge her in a large circle to get her used to having someone on her while she was moving. We wanted to keep her as relaxed as possible while we moved nice and slow. If things went perfect we might try a slow jog toward the end of our first session.

Brad was getting ready to give me a leg up so I could lean over Ella's back as planned. Just as I was getting ready to put my weight on her back she moved her body away leaving me no choice but to come back to the ground and try again. I tried this several more times with the same result.

I looked over at Dusty who was now watching everything we were doing. I spoke to her saying, "When I had asked you to teach her how to be a horse you could have left that part out." She gave me an innocent look. Then she quickly dropped her head down to graze and pretended to ignore us.

We brought Ella over to the fence so we could get her into a position where she could not move away from me as Brad gave me a leg up. She was a tall horse like her sire so Brad had to hoist me up quite quickly before she would move. I landed with a thump on her back. I could feel her tighten up with this new unaccustomed weight on her back. Carol was reassuring her that everything was alright. She relaxed a little and took a couple slow steps forward. We did several short walks with me leaning over her side until she stood still as I mounted from anywhere in the coral. We decided it was time that I actually sit in the saddle. I swung my leg over her, confident that it would be ok, but not completely sure. All at once I was sitting in the saddle on my own horse! She did not resist at all and I was ecstatic! Now that I was sitting on her back we walked her in a circle still attached to the lunge line. She just walked along quietly taking a look every once in a while at me on her back. I patted her neck letting her know what a good girl she was. Things were moving along smoothly and Carol suggested we do a slow jog in both directions and call it a day. I could not have been more proud of Ella. It seemed all the groundwork Brad and I had done with her had really paid off.

Suddenly, Dusty let out a loud squeal and raced to the top of the hill bucking the whole way. The only thing I could think of was that she had been bitten by a bee. Rebel decided he needed to join her leaving his post at the fence. "*Oh no,*" I thought. Ella jumped forward trying to gallop to her friends. Carol was quick to react with a strong grip on the lunge line. She kept Ella moving in a circle, but now it was at a gallop not a walk. I grabbed the neck strap not wanting to pull on Ella's mouth. Carol started talking in a loud calm voice telling me to hang on and ride it out until she calmed down. Ella's long legs covered the ground in the tight circle going round and round so fast I had trouble keeping my seat. After some time she eventually broke to a trot and then a walk and came to a complete halt.

Carol shook her head saying " Well that was unexpected, are you okay? I have to say I never anticipated that happening. I wonder what got into those other horses."

I just looked at her not able to form any words for what had just happened. I was so grateful that she had been on the lunge line. All her expertise had allowed her to stay in control turning a near disaster into a learning experience.

I patted Ella's sweaty neck letting her catch her breath. Brad walked over to me with a big grin on his face teasing, "you wanted to be the first to ride her, guess you won't forget this ride for a long time."

I just looked down at him from Ella's back and shook my head glad that I hadn't fallen off. He helped me off so I didn't bump Ella as I dismounted her. My legs were shaking and almost gave out on me as my feet met the ground. I didn't realize how shaken up I was. Brad was right. I would never forget my first ride on Ella.

I looked over at the fence and there stood Dusty and Rebel with the most innocent looks on their faces.

"I have a mind not to feed you your dinners tonight!" I said to them as I walked out my sweaty horse.

The next sessions went without any complications. I locked both Dusty and Rebel in their stalls just to make sure they would not cause any mischief.

Brad gave me riding lessons on Ella once a week. She was a smart horse with a willing, honest spirit that picked training up easily. We mixed up her work to keep it interesting and fun. We worked on her flat work at home and did some low level dressage shows to keep us focused. We took her cross country schooling, letting her go along with the other horses for the experience not really jumping anything serious. It would be another year before we seriously did any jumping. I was tempted to start her because she showed such a natural ability. But, Brad warned me to be patient because her body wasn't ready for the demands of jumping just yet.

That year we played in the water jumps and sailed over the ditches and galloped the courses just waiting for her to mature before we introduced any serious jumping.

Lucy and I went on many long trail rides that year too. We would cross over the creek and race to the Sister's Woods. Ella loved to run. She always left Dusty way behind. It was pure joy to sit tight on her back and let the speed of her gallop make tears in my eyes. She seemed to enjoy life and wanted to share that joy with me.

Her fourth birthday was coming up and I had decided to take Ella back to the Equestrian Center for more in depth training. Her training was coming along swiftly and having her at the Center would be easier.

It was going to be hard leaving Frank's cozy barn and taking Ella away from Dusty and Rebel. Though she would be less than a mile away it was still a little sad.

I unloaded Ella from the trailer and walked her to her new stall. Lucy had come with me to help get Ella settled. On Ella's new stall door was a shiny name plate and under that was all her information. Lucy had painstakingly put it all together for me as a surprise.

After I had Ella settled I went to put all my equipment away in the tack room. I kept my equipment in an old plastic tub; it wasn't beautiful but it worked. As I walked up to my tack space I noticed a beautiful tack trunk. I thought, "*Oh no someone left their equipment in my space.*" As I walked up to it I noticed that it had my name on it. It was one more gift from Lucy and Frank. I ran my hands over it not believing they had been so generous. Lucy was excited to put my things in it. I let her organize it standing back just soaking up the moment of having such great friends.

Goals

I was excited to use Ella as my Pony Club horse for the upcoming season. I had two years of High School left and wanted to have Ella ready for the for the Young Riders Team by the time she turned six. This had been a proposal Brad had put before me when he saw how much both Ella and I loved eventing.

So, we started to jump Ella that fourth year. She took to it pretty much as we expected with a few moments where I think she questioned our methods. She was tall and teaching her to use that large body in an athletic way was sometimes amusing. When we would ask her to do a course of more than three jumps in a row it proved to be a challenge for her. Her long legs just did not seem to be in the right place to make the jumps. Sometimes she would take off for the fence so far away I just had to sit tight hoping I wouldn't fall off. Other times she would come so close to the base of the fence that at the last moment she would heave her large body up and over coming down with a thud on the other side, making it almost impossible to continue to the next fence. The most promising thing about her training was that she never refused to try.

As she approached her fifth birthday she seemed to grow into herself. All of the sudden the course-work was getting easier for her. She quit putting in the odd steps that made her jump look awkward. She learned to use that large body in a smooth athletic way. Height and depth of jumps suddenly became no problem for her as we challenged her new athletic ability.

She had the best assets of both her mother and father and she loved her job. It seemed everyday Ella and I grew closer. Our trust in each other grew greater as we played on the cross country jump course. I was so proud to be her owner! She had such a big heart. She did everything willingly, was full of courage, and she always tried her best for me.

Brad was true to his word and helped me train her, giving me lessons every week. Then one day after an exceptionally great lesson, he looked at me and said, "I think I should be taking lessons from you. The two of you are a great team."

I patted Ella's neck, looking at Brad like I had not quite heard him right.

Brad continued, "I will help to keep you sharp but to teach you anything new, you need someone more qualified than me."

"You can't mean what you are saying. We have always worked together," I said to Brad. "You have been with us from the beginning. You know Ella almost as well as I do."

"Yes, that is true, that is why I know that you need to get a trainer that has more experience than me to get you to Young Rider Championships. The new trainer in the barn is excellent and he has the experience and expertise to bring you to the next level."

"Let me think about it, but, for now I am happy with the way things are," I said.

"Don't worry, you will never get rid of me." he said with a twinkle in his eye. Can you meet me here tomorrow morning? I would like to take Liam on a nice long trail ride to the falls."

"Sounds like fun! When do you want to meet?"

"After chores late morning"

"Okay I will see you tomorrow late morning"

"Nicole, I want you to think about what I said earlier."

I understood what he was saying, but I felt adrift, like something had shifted in our relationship—something I was not ready to give up. In the Pony Club Clinics I had worked with trainers who were experts in their field. They were always pushing me to make large long-term goals for Ella that were beyond the training I was getting from Brad. I knew that if I chose these goals that I would have to move beyond what he could teach me. Brad and I had talked about these dreams and he always encouraged me to go for them. He reassured me that I wouldn't get rid of him and that he would always be around to keep me in line.

Wequiock Falls

*L*iam had filled out and was brought back to health under Brad's loving care. He was now a beauty with a glossy, dark coat that glistened. You would never know that he was the run-down horse who was kept in the back of the barn to make sure he would live. He had come back to full health and made Brad a wonderful horse.

The day was begging for some fun. There were long stretches along the trail that were perfect to open up our horses and gallop. We were in high spirits, enjoying the horses beneath us that were in the mood for a race. We talked it over, and both of us thought a short hard gallop for Liam would not be too much for him.

There was a tall pine tree that stood alone next to the trail. Brad pointed at it saying, "once we get to the tree I will count down from three. Then I will beat you to the gate that leads to the woods."

I replied, "Let me see you try." The next thing I heard was three, two, one. Both horses exploded beneath us. Ella took the lead, eating up the ground. I could feel Liam gaining on us coming up from behind. I looked to my right side, and there was Liam settling in next to us. He was matching us stride for stride. At that moment I no longer saw Liam as the broken-down horse. I saw the magnificent race horse Smooth Fleet toying with us, loving what he was bred to do. The will to win, his natural speed, and determination had been restored! All the loving attention Brad had painstakingly put into him showed from his eyes that were set on the finish line. In the last five strides before the finish line, Liam maneuvered himself in front of us and won the race!

As we pulled up our horses to go through the gate to the Sister's Woods, I was amazed at the power of love to restore.

"That is not the same horse I first met in the back of the barn," I stated.

"No, he even surprised me. He knew just what to do. All I had to do was hang on and ask for the win at the end," Brad replied as he patted Liam's neck as he pranced through the gate, knowing he had won.

We threaded through the woods that followed the creek to Wequiock Falls Park. We had a lot of rain the week before, so the creek was high and the falls were really flowing. The falls flowed from Wequiock creek into a large ravine. You could get to the base of the falls by following a winding path that was rather steep. The falls had a drop of about twenty-five feet and that day it was roaring. The day was warm with a soft breeze and the first glimpse of leaves were just starting to show on the trees. Spring was in her glory, and the music of the birds filled the air as they flitted from branch to branch.

We worked our way down to the base of the falls. You could feel the spray from the falls on your face. The power of the water was making the horses nervous, so we just stopped there for a short while. As we started to head back to the top, we heard the roar of motorcycles. People came to look at the falls all the time, so I didn't think much about it at first. I looked up to check out who was coming and recognized the faces.

I groaned, "Oh no."

"What?" Brad said.

"It's the guys from school." I said.

"Then you know them. That's good, isn't it?" Brad asked.

"No, those guys are jerks. The one on the red bike keeps asking me out and I put him off by saying I have to work or take care of my horse. That is true, but he hates getting pushed off. I really don't like him."

"Oh," was all Brad said.

We reached the top of the trail across from the lookout parking lot and headed to the hand pump where we were going to give the horses a drink.

The pump was a working historical artifact that had once been used by the stage coaches that had traveled through that area many years ago. The county had kept it in working condition and it was a favorite historical attraction of the park. It was kept under an open roofed shelter that had benches where you could sit and rest. The pump had a large oversized trough under it for the horses to drink out of. It was one of my favorite stops during our long trail ride.

I kept looking over my shoulder hoping the bikers would not notice us. Brad told me not to worry and that they would not bring their bikes onto the grassy area. But, I noticed he was keeping a close eye on them also.

Luck was not on our side that day. They shouted my name and started toward us, leaving the parking lot, riding over the green grassy expanse to the water pump just as we were getting back on our horses. They came way too close to the horses and started to make remarks about the working girl and her horse.

I tried to defuse the moment by laughing at the remark. The leader on the red bike eyed Brad and said in an malicious voice, "Is he the reason you are always so busy?" Then one of them started saying, "Let's see these horses move." Things were escalating out of control fast. They started to rev the engines on their bikes to intimidate us and spook the horses.

I don't know what got into me, but the next thing coming out of my mouth was, "Do you want to see this horse move?"

Motivated by anger, I dug my heels into Ella's sides, and she jumped forward into a full gallop as I circled her and headed toward the jerk on his bike. His eyes widened, and his mouth fell open as he realized all 1,200 pounds of horse and rider was headed straight toward him as he sat on his bike. I asked Ella at the last moment, and we sailed over his head as I took my crop down on his helmet to make my point.

The look on his face was priceless. I turned Ella toward them again.

"She is crazy! Let's get out of here," they yelled as they took off on their bikes.

Brad just sat there calmly and finally said, "Are you finished?" I just stared at him, adrenaline pumping through me not believing what I had just done.

"That was probably one of the most stupid things I have witnessed, but I have to say it was effective. I don't know if I should throttle you or kiss you," he said with exasperation.

I thought a kiss would be nice. Instead of voicing my feelings I grabbed his helmet, pulled it over his eyes, and cantered off down the trail toward the barn.

Klaus

Spring turned to early summer. Ella was usually waiting at the gate for me when I would come to the barn. She seemed to sense when I would be coming and always greeted me with a warm nicker. We had a routine that after I had her halter on her she, would stretch out her neck asking me to scratch her favorite sweet spot. I usually indulged her just to watch the enjoyment she got from it. If I rubbed it good and hard her top lip would begin to quiver which always made me laugh.

I had decided to prepare for an upper level certificate for our Pony Club and was going to also try to qualify for the Young Rider Championships that year. It was going to be a busy summer! Just the way I liked it.

That meant there were going to be many riding clinics to help me prepare for the upcoming events. At Pony Club clinics we had to switch horses with the other riders. When Ella saw me riding another horse she would pin her ears at that horse and try to turn her back on them as if to say, " she is mine stay away." It always made me laugh but a part of me loved her for it. I attended every clinic our club had to offer. I also started to teach riding lessons to pay for my expenses for Ella too. My students were more than happy to let me ride their horses to get ready for my ambitious goals.

I took a pre-exam to evaluate my riding and it showed some weaknesses that I had to correct if I wanted to pass. I needed another set of eyes on the ground to help me overcome my problem. It could not just be anyone either. They had to be someone with the keen ability to get me to the standard. I have no idea how I had gotten so far without anyone pointing out my riding shortcomings. I think it was because Ella was such a great athlete that she covered up where I lacked. It had taken the very experienced rater to spot my weaknesses during the pre-exam. But, the real live exam was in six weeks so I needed help fast. I was feeling quite desperate that there might not be enough time to correct my riding.

Brad and Carol took me out to dinner after the pre-exam and we poured over the rater's comments together. Many good things were said, especially about Ella, but the last comment on the sheet was about some inconsistency in the way I sat in the saddle that would make it impossible to pass if not corrected. I talked with the rater and got some good pointers on things I could do to improve my seat, but whether there was enough time for me to correct the way I had always rode was a worrisome question.

Carol asked me if I would consider working with the new trainer at the barn. She said she could put a word in for me. Brad just looked at me with raised eyebrows as if to say, "*I told you so.*" Time was short. I had worked too hard to quit now, but the new trainer at the barn was not my first choice. I knew time was not on my side and I thought, *What do I have to lose?*

The trainer who taught at the barn was a former olympian rider from Germany. He had a loud voice with a thick accent that really carried. No matter where you were in the arena you could hear him loud and clear. He was already teaching advanced dressage to a few of the riders at the barn. At the times I observed him teaching I always felt glad that he was not my trainer. Not because he didn't have amazing results, but he was always so gruff with the riders. I always wondered why they would take a second lesson from him. There just had to be more to him than I had observed. I knew he knew his stuff because no one makes it to the Olympics without outstanding skill. I was getting desperate and I needed someone of his caliber to help me. Dressage was my weak point, and it was his strong suit, so I thought I would give him a try.

I noticed that he kept his critical eye on Ella as we worked in the arena. He never said anything to me so I just sort of ignored him best I could. Carol talked with Klaus and told him what I was up against. He agreed to evaluate me and see if he could help.

We started the next day 8:00 a.m. sharp. He was waiting in the riding arena with a copy of my evaluation in his hand and a copy of the test. As I came into the arena I noticed that he had set up a small, difficult jump course that was meant to test our ability.

He came up to me as I entered the arena. He introduced himself, telling me that he had talked with Carol and would give me an honest evaluation and let me know if he could help me with the amount of time we had left.

The warm up became part of the lesson. That was something I usually did on my own. I would do a little walking, some trot work, and call it done. Klaus taught me that at the level of work I was going to ask of Ella, the warmup was probably just as important as jumping a six-foot fence. A good warmup saved you and your horse from injury. He stressed to me that I should never let anyone rush me into work. We never started our work until Ella's back was warmed up with a good swinging trot. From that day forward, I was always in the arena at least a half hour before my lesson so that when Klaus walked into the arena, we were warmed up and ready to work.

That first day he had me go through a series of exercises without saying much to me. He would watch, raise his eyebrows, shake his head, and then write down something on the sheet he was holding. I was starting to get anxious. Without any feedback, I started to wonder what he was thinking, and anger rooted in the fear of failure started to raise within me. Ella and I had always been told we were a great team. *Who was this grouchy old man, anyway?* I thought.

After the last exercise was finished, he called me into the center of the arena. As I walked up to him he kept his eyes on my pre-exam paper. I waited until he finally looked up at me. With his head tilted and one eyebrow arched, he said to me, "You like to jump," more as a statement than a question. "This mare could jump the moon for you. Her natural athletic ability makes everything easy, and you have developed a bad habit in your flat work that will never take away from your jumping, but will always hinder your dressage work."

"I have been watching this horse since I arrived to this barn. She is the most athletic horse I've seen in years. Her style is classic. Horses like these are very rare. To tell you the truth, I agreed to take a look at you because I like your horse. She is ready for this test. As for you, I believe we can get you to this level with extremely hard work. But to be at this level in six weeks is a question that only time will tell. We have to focus on new muscle memory so that even if you get tense during the exam, you don't go back to your old ways. I noticed when you got angry with me for not giving you feedback, you tensed up. We have to overcome that. You are good rider, but this test demands excellence. Never start working until you know that horse is listening and completely warmed up. For the next six weeks, you are never to rush and always finish the ride so that the horse feels like it has done its job for you. It is important to quit on a high note, especially when you are introducing new movements. Always go back to something that is easy for them so that they like their work. This is a partnership; it is like a dance, and you are the lead in this dance. You must know where you are going and what you expect of your partner. Never start a session without a clear picture of what you want to accomplish for that day. Now may I ride your mare? I would like to show you something that you need to see."

Not many other riders had ridden Ella, and I had never seen him ride. I had only heard of what he had accomplished in the horse world. I knew one ride would not hurt her, so I agreed.

He mounted her and walked her on a long rein, talking to me as he made his way around the arena. He had a flawless seat, and Ella's ears were already tuned into what was expected of her. Her walk lengthened out, and her step became deeper and more athletic.

"She is already warmed up, so I will show you some simple patterns that will create deeper collection that demands a correct seat. He asked Ella for a trot and developed it into something I did not think was possible. She looked as if she was floating as she covered the ground. He kept changing speed and degrees of collection. Ella was totally focused on him. He was completely quiet up there but getting transitions from walk to canter that I had never gotten out of her. All of the sudden, he broke away from the rail, and all I can say is that they were dancing. It was astounding to watch. Ella was his partner, and they were dancing together with such ease and rhythm that it seemed they were part of one another.

The moment was over, and just like that he was handing me her reins. He patted her neck, looking at me and telling me I had done a nice job training her but that she had untapped ability.

I was humbled. I could not have gotten Ella even close to moving like that. He was right; I did need to see what he had shown me. It inspired me to keep going. I was not sure what the next six weeks was going to be like, but I knew one thing. I had found the right person to get me there. We had one thing in common; we both liked my horse, and that was enough for me.

"Now go give her a good rub down. She did some work that is going to make her sore. We will start tomorrow with you and see if we can get you up to your horse's level; 8:00 sharp," he said as he walked out of the arena.

I just stared at his back, wondering what I had gotten myself into. It was clear he liked my horse, but I was on the waiting list to get his approval.

"Come on, girl, we better do as he says, but I think you won't be the only one that is going to need a rub down after our lesson tomorrow," I said as I walked toward the wash stall.

I put Ella out to pasture for the day. The first thing she did as I let her go was to lay down, roll on her back, and give herself a good rub. She got up, shook herself off, gave me a good looking over, and then suddenly spun around to join her herd for the day. I laughed and thought, not for the first time, what an incredible gift she was.

I ran into Carol in the lounge, and she asked what I thought about Klaus. She had watched the lesson and had been quite impressed. She warned me, "He is a man of few words, but the words he does use he means. Don't let him bully you, but do ask questions when you don't understand what he wants of you. He will respect that." I told her I had agreed to work with him to get me through this test but was not sure if I would survive the next six weeks. We laughed about the bruises I would incur on the outside and inside.

Ella thrived on all the attention I was giving her. She would be waiting for me ready for her early morning workouts nickering to me as I entered the barn to get her. I always gave her a good brushing rubbing her back and going over her legs to make sure they were not sore.

At 7:30, I entered the arena and started my warm up. At 8:00 sharp, Klaus entered the arena. This became the pattern for the next six weeks. Even if I did not have a scheduled ride with Klaus, he would be there watching and growling when he didn't like what he saw. Pretty soon I heard that growl whenever I moved in a wrong direction, even when he wasn't there. It was uncanny how he had gotten in my head. I thought to myself that I had better watch it, or I would start talking with a German accent.

On my first lesson, he took away my stirrups and put Ella on a lunge line. He had Ella move out into a trot. I had no stirrups, no reins, and had only my balance and leg to keep me on her as we went around a twenty-meter circle. He wanted to isolate my seat and leg without the use of stirrups or reins. This put me in the correct position and allowed me to focus on my seat without having to focus on anything else. He told me exactly where to put my leg and where I was to sit on her back that allowed her the ability to move with ease. Every time I did it right, he would say, "Ya!" And every time I didn't, he growled, "*No!*" I got to the point on the lunge line where I heard more *ya's* than *no's*. Finally, he took me off the lunge line and gave me my reins. I was to walk to the rail and cue Ella for a trot. As I was cueing Ella to walk forward, I heard the growl and moved to my correct position without him saying a word. Quickly came the *ya*, and we were moving forward.

During that lesson, he taught me more about training than I had learned in all of the years of my riding combined. He taught me how to get a horse listening to you by using your leg and seat effectively. I learned that any movement on top of the horse can affect the movement of the horse under you. The trick was to get them tuned in to what was being asked. Most horses just learn to ignore the rider most of the time. We were teaching Ella to listen to the slightest movement. If I raised my shoulder or moved my head, that was a cue she was to get ready for me to ask for something. By the end of the lesson, I was beginning to feel when I came out of position and would self-correct. He would pressure me asking for multiple transitions and every time I would slip into my old way, I would hear the *no* and would quickly correct and wait for the *ya*.

Each lesson we would talk about our plan for my ride that day and how I was to execute it and what my backup plan would be if that did not work. He stressed the idea that you must always have a plan. You had to know when to back off and when to ask for more. Anyone can ride, but not everyone can train. I wanted to train, so I soaked up every bit of information he gave me.

By the end of the fourth week, I had been riding so much the inside of my legs had open blisters. There was no time to slow down and back off if I was to reach my goal. Each day I would wrap my legs and then put on my half chaps and pray they would not get infected. Each night I took a hot bath and soaked my wounds, putting ointment on them to keep infection from setting in. I didn't dare tell my mother or anyone else for fear they would have me back off. I could let them heal after the test. One day Klaus saw me adjusting my half chap and must have been able to see that I was in pain. He demanded to see the sores. Before he could say anything, I begged him not to tell anyone. I promised I would let them heal after the test. He shook his head and made me promise I would take care of them and if they got infected I would see a doctor.

Klaus came into the arena at the end of the fifth week with my stirrups. He handed them to me and said, "We have one week to go. Let's see how you do with these back. I think you will be surprised at how independent you have become."

I have to admit it felt awkward at first to have them back. By the end of the fifth week, I was riding at a level I had not thought was possible. No longer did I hear any growling. I was teaching Ella to dance with me.

The Test

The day of the Pony Club test had arrived. Brad and Carol were my support system. Brad kept giving me a hard time to keep my nerves steady. I think he was more nervous than I was. I was not sure if he was a comfort or just a pain. I was so focused, and every thought had a slight German accent to it. Klaus did not come. He said I did not need him. Ella was in great shape, and my poor legs only had to last one more day.

I had read through the test so many times I had it memorized. The assessors would be looking for in-depth knowledge and ability in the following criteria: outside riding, over fences, cross country, indoor riding, lunging, and training the young horse.

These were the areas I had been living and breathing with single focus for the last six weeks. Klaus had studied the test, found my weaknesses, and turned them into strengths in a way that gave me a confidence in my ability. He had taught me how to focus and analyze what was in front of me, to map out a usable plan, and execute it. His critical eye and expansive knowledge kept me focused and always reaching for more.

The day of the test was a gray day with a slight drizzle. Brad and Carol had come with me for moral support. They would not be able to talk to me until the test was finished, but it was a comfort to know that they were there.

I pulled on my slicker and found Ella a stall. There were four of us taking the test-one boy and three girls, all from different parts of the United States and Canada. Everyone was friendly, but one girl stood out. Her nickname was Red. She got that name from the mass of deep red hair that crowned her head. She had a friendly smile and inquisitive eyes that took in everything. She loved to talk, and I liked to listen, so the two of us hung together through the day, encouraging each other.

The day started out with a briefing in a dusty barn lounge that had three large tabby cats draped over old couches, waiting for you to sit down so they could jump in your lap for a good pet. They purred soothingly as we mindlessly petted them as we listened to assessors. They went over the rules and we were all very attentive to what they had to say.

After the briefing, Red and I headed to the barn to get our horses and saddle up.

The first portion of the test was riding on the flat. All flat work was done without stirrups. For the first time, I was glad Klaus had made me ride all those weeks without them. Ella was extra attentive to everything. It was as if she realized that we were being tested, and she was going to let them know that she could meet the challenge. My confidence began to soar as I warmed her up. Ella had always delighted in a crowd and worked harder when she was being watched. She began to dance beneath me making all the movements expected of her to look effortless. Her flat work had become our greatest strength.

Red watched our workout, waiting her turn. As I came out of the arena, she gave me a high five and said, "You can be on my team anytime."

I laughed and said, "good luck" as she passed me to do her portion of the flat work. I stayed and watched her. She was a good strong rider and a pleasure to watch. As she came out of the arena I said to her, "I would be honored to be on any team she was on." We both laughed and headed to the barn to rub our horses down and prepare for the next part of the test.

I sat outside of Ella's stall on a bail of hay where one of the tabby cats found my lap and decided to take a nap purring as I was cleaning my bridle.

"Looks like you found a friend," Red said as she sat next to me and gave the cat a scratch on the top of it head. She had been outside watching them set the course for the second part of the test.

"They have finished putting the course together. It's time to saddle up. Can you do me a favor?" she asked.

"What is that?" I replied.

"You go first, make it look real easy so I'm not so nervous."

"I will do my best for you Red," I laughed.

We turned to our horses to saddle them. Ella had her head over the door staring into the gray day. She stood motionless barely breathing, her ears pricked forward as if she was studying the fences that were across the yard that were waiting for her to jump. She was usually so curious and active and this stillness was new to me. I wasn't sure what to make of it. "What's up girl," I asked looking in the same direction she was. "I know how you feel," I said. As as I saddled her up I reassured her and myself that we were ready for this. I waited for Red telling her that if they would let me I would be happy to go first.

"I hate waiting. I'm no good at it. I want to get this done," I said as I zipped up my coat against the drizzle that was beginning to come down.

This part of the test was riding over fences without stirrups. I was able to be the first rider over the fences. Before I started to work I calmed myself, visualizing each fence with Ella clearing them with ease as my body stayed in the correct position, guiding my partner. This was done in a large outdoor arena that had great footing. We worked over cavalettis, gymnastic fences, and stadium fences. The height of the stadium fences were set at the maximum height for Ella and me. All that work that Klaus had made me do without my stirrups had really paid off.

"You didn't have to make it look quite that easy," Red said as I finished that portion of the test.

"Well I was only doing what you asked me to do Red," I said in a teasing way.

The confidence I showed on the outside didn't match the pressure I had building on the inside. I was glad this portion of the test was behind me.

The next portion of the test was riding in the open over cross country jumps. The dark skies had decided to open up with a nice steady rain. The ground was getting slippery. As a precaution I put studs in Ella's shoes so she wouldn't slip. The studs should act like track shoes giving extra traction that would be needed over the wet ground. We had only used studs on her shoes a few times and I was a little reluctant to use them for the test. I wasn't sure if they would mess up her rhythm. I didn't want to take a chance of her slipping and hurting herself so I put them on. I developed a good strong rhythmic gallop checking how the studs would work. They worked just as they were designed to not interfering with Ella's balance.

Once I was sure of our footing I started off for the first part of the course that led into the woods where a nice straightforward log fence met us that led to a ditch that Ella sailed over landing in mud that would have given way under her if not for the studs in her shoes. As we came out of the woods into a open field the rain stopped and the sun started to peek behind the clouds. In the field we encountered a steep bank with a sheer drop that led to a water jump, and then onto a couple sets of combination jumps. Ella moved over the ground jumping fences with great confidence as if this was just a schooling course that she had done many times. She still had plenty of energy as we finished the course. I loosened the feel I had on the reins and let her prance, patting her neck and letting her know how proud I was of her.

For the last portion of the test, we were given a horse that we had never seen and were expected to come up with a plan on the spot that would improve the horse's way of going. The horse that was assigned to me reminded me of Dusty when I had first started to ride her. She was older and cranky and full of burrs. The first thing I did was clean her up taking the burs from her mane and tail. It was obvious that she had never been trained properly. She shied at things in the arena and did not want to pay attention to me. I needed to get her attention or the test would be over for me. I took a ground pole and placed it in the center of the arena at an angle just as Brad had done for me with Dusty so many years ago. The first thing I trained her to do was to stand still as

I mounted her. This took several attempts, but she finally got it. I made sure she responded to the pressure on the bit, by slowing down. Once I was sure she understood that I worked at getting her attention on the rail by doing multiple transitions from walk to trot to canter. After that I introduced the ground pole in the center of the arena. She spooked at it, throwing herself away from it and almost unseating me. I slipped off her back and walked her over the ground pole, letting her get a good look at it. She snorted and smelled it and finally decided that it wasn't going to eat her. I led her over it several times, letting her follow me until she did it without hesitation. I re mounted her and started the exercise just as I had done that first day in the Sister's Woods with Brad. It worked wonderfully. As the day continued to progress, my focus stayed sharp, and I was able to evaluate and comment appropriately on each horse and rider.

Now all I had to do was wait for the results. Over an hour had passed and there were still no results. Then someone said that two riders had passed, one got a partial pass, and one failed.

I could not help nervously pacing. Ella had been flawless. I felt pretty confident but one never knows what is in an assessor's mind. Finally, each one of us was individually called to the office to go over their test. The first person to be called was the girl from Canada who was three years older than me.

She was in the room for what seemed like forever. When she finally came out, she was barely holding back tears. She just walked past us without a word. We all knew what that meant. She did not pass.

Red, the most aggressive rider in our group at that point, stood up and said, "Enough! I can't wait any longer," and walked into the office without being called. I thought for sure they would kick her out of there, but she must have done some fast talking because the door did not open. After a few minutes I heard a jubilant "*Yes!*" come from the room and then she appeared all smiles with one of the assessors right behind her, warning us to wait until our name was called. Everything within me wanted to get this over.

The boy next to me was biting his fingernails. He looked at me and said, "It's me, I know. I blew that part of the test, and you were the best rider out there." I shook my head. He was a good rider and trainer. He had good instincts and you can never tell what is running through an assessor's head. All of a sudden, his name was called, and I was alone in the waiting room with my thoughts. He was in there for quite a while, and when the door finally opened, my eyes focused on his to see if I could read the answer to what waited for me behind that door. His eyes did not give away any answers. He just gave me a half smile and nodded his head as he exited. As the door shut, I stood up and started to pace. What was taking so long? Finally, the door opened and I was ushered into the small office.

The test sat on the table before me but before I could pick it up, they started the debrief with a short speech about the test. This little speech continued, but for the life of me I could not have cared less. I just wanted to hear the results.

All of the sudden, my ears started to hear things like; we have not seen an eye like yours in a long time, well executed plans, and wonderful seat. My head shot up and my ears tuned into what they were saying. I just sat there with a grin on my face, not saying a word. They all stood and shook my hand with comments such as, "You have a wonderful future ahead of you, outstanding job."

As they left, I just sat back in my chair and closed my eyes. I thanked the good Lord once again for his divine providence for the people he had brought into my life and most of all for Ella.

Brad and Carol were waiting for me at the barn next to Ella's stall. I kept a straight face, said nothing, and started to straighten up the equipment and get ready for the long ride home. I think they were afraid to ask the outcome of the test. Finally, Brad said, "Well, it couldn't have been that bad." I took the test handed it to him and said, 'The test speaks for itself."

Brad went straight to the last page and read out loud, "Passed," Carol grabbed the test out of his hand and started reading out loud all the wonderful comments that were on those pages.

I turned looking at them with a smile and eyes filled with tears. "I couldn't have done this without you. You are both such a blessing to me. I don't have the words to express how much I appreciate you both."

After that little speech was when the party began. Brad poured a bucket of water over my head that broke all the emotional tension and we started to laugh. The other candidates came over and we said our goodbyes.

When Red came over, she threw her arm around me, saying she was trying out for the Young Riders Championships and would see me at the camp. We exchanged information. I looked forward to spending more time getting to know her.

As we pulled into the barn there in the middle of the driveway stood Klaus. His face was blank and his eyes were serious. We stopped next to him, rolled down the window, and Carol said, "Hi, Klaus." She then handed the test to him without another word. Just as Brad had done, he went to the last page. The serious eyes began to twinkle and his face now had a small smile on it. All I heard was "Ya" as he handed the test back to Carol. Without another word, he turned away from us and started down the driveway toward the barn whistling.

Preparations

Over the next couple of weeks I gave the open sores on my legs time to heal. All the riding I did was bareback. It was wonderful not to have to worry about anything but enjoying flying down the trails with Ella each morning. We would race to the top of the knoll and together we watched the sunrise. I would slip off her bridle and hand graze her soaking in the wonder of a new day and the friendship of this wonderful animal. I would lay my head on her side and just soak in her friendship. I wanted these days to last forever.

The rest of the summer lay ahead of me with college starting in the fall. My mother was putting pressure on me to make some hard decisions with Ella. I kept putting off the reality of what that would entail but the pressure was beginning to build as the date to start college came closer. I had decided to go to school to become a veterinarian. Enjoying lazy summer days before I would have to take on years of hard work looked enticing.

"Brad, I am thinking of just slowing down the pace and enjoying the rest of the summer without the pressure of shows and the thought of possible championships."

"What's bringing on this change of mind? Ella is in great shape and ready for the challenge," he reassured me.

"It's not that. Mom is after me to make some choices about Ella before school starts. Just the thought of it breaks my heart. If I make the young riders team for championships we would use up the whole summer training. I'm not sure I want to spend our last days together with that kind of pressure."

"I thought this is something you wanted?"

"It is, but to be honest I will have to do some extremely intense training. I am still having trouble with the Trakehner and that stupid Coffin jump."

"You have time to work on these. They are just new to to you and Ella."

"I know, but time is passing so fast I just want to stop it and slow it down. Going off to start school without Ella is tearing me up."

"I wish I could help you with Ella. Ever since Ella was a young foal you have have talked about making the Young Riders team."

"That was just a young girl's dream."

"Yes, it may have been a dream but you have the chance to actually make it a reality. Right now you have the time and the right horse. This opportunity may never come your way again. I think you need to seriously think about this. What does Klaus have to say about this?"

"I don't know I think he is waiting for me to make up my mind"

"I'm sure he is in the barn somewhere. Let's go talk with him."

Klaus was just finishing up a lesson with a new student. Watching him teach still amazed me. He could get more out of a horse and rider than anyone I had ever seen. It was just an inspiration to watch him. After he had finished with the lesson I talked with him about all the thoughts that I had rolling around in my head about Ella. It was such a relief to finally voice my fears to someone I trusted with Ella and my heart.

When I finished he looked at me with kindness in his eyes. "This is your decision you have to make it and live with it. I can't make time stand still but one thing I know is that if you don't try for this you will never know if it was possible and that you might regret. If you chose to go for it there will be challenges but that is something you have never backed away from."

I stood looking at him for a moment then said, "let's go for it."

Klaus smiled at me grabbing his calendar to set up a training schedule.

Brad punched the air yelling,"Yes!"

Klaus and I worked side by side the rest of the summer. We mapped out Ella's training schedule and then started down the road toward the goal to get us qualified for the championships. Many days were spent on the cross-country course going over the jumps that included the next level of difficulty that we would encounter. He would have me walk the grounds each day visualizing going over every jump. We talked about each jump: the correct way to approach it, what to do if my approach wasn't perfect, and most importantly what to do if I found myself struggling. He stressed the importance of keeping your head in the game to keep both you and your horse safe. Speed, balance, and control were always being checked as I made my way to each combination of obstacles around the course. Many of the jump combinations were new to both Ella and myself. Jumping at this level unprepared could put us both in danger. Even though she had the ability, we needed to train her and not push her so fast that we hurt her confidence. It was a delicate balance of moving up and not overextending Ella's inexperience. We were learning this together and I had to rely on Klaus to get us through this safely.

Klaus assured me that Ella was ready. We had practiced the "Skinny," a very narrow jump, until I was assured that I could keep Ella straight through this narrow jump. Ella also became brave over the very difficult trakehner jump. She always slightly over jumped it so I had to make sure I hung on tight. It was the coffin jump that always gave me trouble. I usually approached it in a fast flat gallop and missed my striding, either causing Ella to refuse or me to fall. The jump had three elements to it that had to be thought of as one continuous movement or you just couldn't make it through successfully. It really tested the rider's skill. Out of all the jumps this is the one that Klaus made me visualize the most. I needed to adjust Ella's canter enough to make it over the first rail, then the ditch and then up and over the last set of rails. I had to see it, but I also had to feel it or that jump was going to cause us trouble.

I had to place high in several upcoming Events if I was going to qualify for the regional team. Now the time had come to test all our training at an Event and see how we would do.

The day of that event came on a perfect summer morning, slightly cool from the night air promising to warm up as the day progressed. The grounds had open sweeping hills with large pine trees that dotted the course.

I was ready for the dressage and show jumping portion of the test, but the cross country course always had questions that had to be addressed before we jumped them. Klaus went over every jump with me having me repeat back how I was going to negotiate the course. There was a dreaded coffin jump that was part of the course. It had an option route that you could use skipping the coffin jump all together. If I chose to use it I would incur penalty points but that would be better than failing the jump altogether.

I backed Ella into the starting box as they counted the final three, two, one. She shot out of the box way too fast. I pulled on the reins coming up to the first fence flat barely making it over. We continued forward but never got a nice rhythm going. All the fences seemed to come up too fast. We had a refusal at one fence and had to re approach. The dreaded coffin jump was coming up and I was coming in on it way too fast and flat to make it through. I took the option route knowing I would have penalty points, but would just be happy to make it through the rest of the course.

The cross country portion of the test wasn't pretty but we had made it through allowing us to do the show jumping the next day.

Klaus and Brad met me at the finish line of the cross country course. "How did it go?" Klaus asked.

"Did you see the first jump? The rest of the course went the same way. We never got a nice rhythm going. Ella jumped everything but it wasn't very pretty."

"Good! Now we know what to focus on."

"Oh."

"Ella has heart and is brave. We can teach her rhythm. The other thing we need to work on are your nerves. She feeds off you and if you are unsure you run into trouble."

Now our schooling became all about the rhythm of the course and how each fence was connected to the next to make it look smooth and easy. Yet, I was still coming in too flat on the coffin jump. This would make us land too long over the first fence and that gave us no room to do the rest of the fences. Because we never got it quite right during training I would always take the option route at Events.

Klaus looked at me hard saying,"Nicole, Ella can do the coffin jump. We just have to make you believe that you can get her through it. If you make it to Championships you will not have the option to skip that fence."

"I know, I know. Let's school it again."

Because I placed well in all of the Events that summer I qualified to tryout for the Young Riders. I did this even though I never did jump the coffin jump at an actual Event. I always took the option route around it.

Qualifying meant a week's worth of camp that evaluated both the horse and rider. I was part of Area IV and they had some of the best riders in the circuit. There were six of us who had qualified for the tryouts and only four were going to make the team as riders. The two that did not make the team as riders would be grooms for the team. Each of us had to demonstrate not only excellence in riding, but we had to also function as a team. It helped a little that I already knew two of the riders. Red from the Pony Club test was here and she was a fabulous cross-country rider. Her weak point was dressage, though she still was a tough competitor in all areas. The other girl was Rebecca from my own local Pony Club. She's the one who had given me the nickname of Charity. She was sweet to my face but, with her I had to watch my back. She liked to win and had no qualms about running you over to get there. She was riding a horse that was experienced at this level. That was Ella's weakness; she had the ability but did not have the experience of the other horses that were at the camp.

The camp was five days long and staffed with great instructors and wonderful volunteers. I was so relaxed and having so much fun. Unfortunately, I was not as focused as I should have been. On the last day of the camp we did a mock run-through of what we would be up against at championships. Ella felt wonderful; she was healthy, energetic, confident, strong, and flexible beneath me. She was amazing in the dressage test. We flew through cross country, but when it came to stadium jumping, I totally lost my focus. I was joking with the others, not worried about what I had to do. Normally, I would have walked the course, visualized the approach to each combination of jumps, and measured the speed I needed to easily fly over the jumps.

I took a look at the course that was posted by the entrance and thought, *No problem*. I entered the arena, did my courtesy circle, and started on the course. We easily maneuvered through the first set of jumps, but then all of the sudden, I was not sure of the rest of the course and had to pull Ella up. You could have heard a pin drop, and my heart dropped into the pit of my stomach. What had I done! I knew better! Ella deserved better. I just sat there seeing my dream slipping away. I had taken for granted that Ella could do anything, but she needed me to keep my head in the game and I had let her down. It was one thing to catch a rail or come into a combination flat, but to just forget the course was unforgivable. I made my way toward the gate with my head down.

Rebecca, the girl from my club, said sweetly, "Sorry about that, Charity," as she passed me entering into the stadium finishing with a perfect round.

At the end of the day, the teams were posted, and my name was not on it. I was posted as an alternate. In the meantime, I would be a groom for the team.

The ride home was very quiet and long except for the occasional deep sigh I let out. I had decided to let myself lick my wounds on the ride home, but once I got out of that truck I was determined to pull myself up and be the best groom they had ever seen. I did not know how I would face Klaus. Carol must have called ahead and let him know what had happened. He was there waiting, I had dried my tears and was trying to put a brave face on my disappointment. He looked at me, and all he said was "Well?" I burst into tears, and he opened his arms to me and let me cry my disappointment out. After the tears were spent he looked at me and said teasing, "Good thing you can clean a saddle and carry water," taking the sting out of my hurt. We both laughed and started to unload the trailer and put Ella to bed for the night.

The championships were six weeks away. I kept Ella fresh and in shape by going on long, slow gallops in the early mornings. We played in the lake and went to a small show to keep us sharp.

Two weeks later, I got a call from the young riders' coach. One of the horses had taken a jump badly and was hurt. Both horse and rider would not be able to perform. I was now a rider on the team.

At that moment everything changed. I went from the role of groom that carried no real pressure to a rider who had to contribute to a team score.

Championships

Ella was in good shape, but we had to sharpen our ability to take large jump combinations at higher speeds. There was always the risk for error the faster you went. We could not go into the jump combination with so much speed that we could not make the turn into the next one. It was all about controlled speed and focus. I still had not taken the coffin jump at a show and it worried me in the back of my mind. We were getting better at it while schooling but it was still a challenge.

I was also a little concerned about how my teammates would accept me. It was one thing to be a groom and another to be someone you depended on in a competition. They had all seen my lapse in judgment on the day of tryouts. But, the first time I got together with them as the new rider. all seemed to be forgiven. The only one who did not fully except me was Rebecca, the girl from my club. She had told the team about how I was given Ella and all the help I was given to train her. I'm not sure why that bothered her so much, but she never seemed to let it go. Most people thought it

was a great story, and my nickname of Charity continued to follow me. Most meant it in an endearing
way, but when Rebecca said it, it always twisted
my guts a little. The unfortunate thing was she was
the captain of the team, so I had to be extra careful.

My greatest ally on the team was Red. She
always had a good word for me and encouraged me.
She was a bold rider if not just a little reckless. Her
horse had a lot of experience at this level and was
a good match for her. She was always the first to
go and the way she rode made me hold my breath.
After she would finish a particularly hard combination, she would trot past me and say, "you can
breathe now." That always made me laugh and took
the edge off the pressure I was putting on myself.

Barbara was the the fourth rider on our team she
was was a good steady rider that seemed unflappable. She was quiet with strong determination that
expressed itself with a sure calm attitude. Unlike Red
and Rebecca she kept her opinions to herself. She
was easy to get along with. With everyone's nerves
stretched from the pressure, that was a real asset
to our team.

As the weeks progressed the team grew closer
and our coach continued to evaluate us to see
where our order of go would be for each leg of the
competition. The one thing our coach was worried
about was the lack of experience Ella and I had at
this level. She seemed harder on us, but I could not

blame her. After all, I was the girl that forgot her course. It must have looked like I didn't care.

My confidence in Ella grew stronger as the time of the competition grew closer. She became stronger and bolder in everything that was put before her. My game plan was to stay out of trouble. I would take no risks, keep my team safe, and most of all, memorize all of my courses.

The first day of National Championships finally came! The day was warm and clear. There were people and horses swarming all around. I could hardly believe that I was there. How did this really happen? Rebecca was right; there was no way a poor girl from Bay Settlement should be on these grounds, much less competing at a national level. Nevertheless, I was there, and I had a job to do.

Our team stayed close to each other and our coach kept our focus on what lay ahead.

The first part of the competition was dressage. Nerves were high, and these horses were in top shape, so keeping them and us focused was a battle.

Ella felt like a coiled spring underneath me. If I breathed wrong, she was more than ready to explode. I used all the training and every trick I had to get her under control and listening to me. I was so focused that when they called my name to enter the arena it came as a surprise.

My coach looked up at me before I entered the arena and asked, "Do you know your test?"

I nodded my head. Dressage was one of Ella's strengths and the team was depending on me for a good score. We boldly entered the arena confident and strong. Ella had tuned into me making each movement of the test look effortless. She floated over the ground doing flawless transitions that not even Klaus could have found fault with. After we finished, I wrapped my arms around her and whispered my thanks.

The rest of the morning I walked the cross-country course studying each fence. It was a beautiful course almost three miles long that ran along the Lake Michigan coast. There were trails through the woods that would open up onto beautiful vistas of the Great Lake. It was a long, hilly course that would take a lot out of the horses and make them tired. The fifth fence was the coffin jump. Just as Klaus had said, there was no alternative route. I would have to jump it. I visualized in my mind's eye Ella clearing each fence with room to spare and finishing in record time. Hopefully, my ride would be as good as my vision. I became so focused I couldn't even talk to anyone. Not even Red could make me laugh. I kept seeing fence five, the coffin jump, waiting for me. I just could not feel it and sometimes as I visualized it we crashed through it and got eliminated. I would quickly change the vision counting out loud the strides needed to take the jump successfully just as Ella and I had done in practice.

Red was the first to ride the course for our team. We watched her clear her first fence then lost her as she made her way into the woods. Barbara and I ran to the top of the hill that allowed us to see her take the coffin jump without any trouble. We then ran to the finish line where we would get the report on how she felt the course ran.

There were twenty-four jumps with some jumps having two or three parts, making a total of thirty-two efforts. Before she dismounted she started her report on the course. The first four fences flowed well, making it easy to establish a good forward gallop with rhythm. Fence five is tricky because it seems to come up fast as you got to the top of the hill. The middle of the course rode well with a tight jump on fence ten, the corner jump, which was made up of two jumps that were not in a straight line. If you came in too fast on the first jump, you could not make the tight turn needed to get to the second jump because you had too much momentum and not enough space to jump the second half of the element. She had to re-approach by circling her horse and getting back up to speed, losing valuable time and accumulating faults. The water complex had good footing and could be ridden at a good fast clip. She also told us to watch out for jump sixteen at the bottom of a hill. It seemed to surprise her horse so much that it slowed down, almost losing the power he needed to get over the jump. They got over with no faults with the good use of her leg, kicking and yelling to get through the jump. Not pretty, but it was effective. The last four jumps were straight-forward through the woods that acted like a shoot, and if you needed to make up time that was a good place to do it.

The next rider to go was Rebecca. She had a good run with one refusal. Her horse had also backed off on jump sixteen and she saved it by taking the optional route.

Barbara was the third rider to go. Cross Country jumping was her horse's strongest phase of the Event. She went clean jumping all the fences without any faults.

I was the last to run for our team. I backed into the timer's box as they were counting backward: five, four, three, two, one. Ella sprung from the box as if she was on a race course! I needed to rein her in and get control if I was to finish this course. I pulled the reins and sat back in the saddle to get her into a slower pace, and thankfully, she responded. We established a strong forward gallop with good rhythm a few strides just before the first jump flying over it, and from there on she settled in as if she was a part of me. There were three jumps in the pine forest that we sailed over. As we came out of the woods we had a steep ride up a hill that opened up to a vista that overlooked Lake Michigan.

There it was, fence five, the coffin jump, and it was coming up fast. I was coming up to it with too much speed. I needed to correct my speed. I pulled on the reins and Ella responded shorting up her stride. I started to talk out loud as we approached the fence counting three strides before the fence. "Three, two, one, up and over the first part of the fence, one stride, over the ditch, one stride up and over the last part of the fence." We cleared it and made it look easy. I was elated! We had some tricky fences coming up but, I knew I could count on Ella to clear them if I kept my head. As we approached jump sixteen I could feel her starting to slow down to get a look at the fence. I put my leg on her asking her to trust me. I felt her respond with more power as I prepared her to take the jump. We finally came to the last four jumps entering back into the cool pine woods that had a nice flat trail. I rode strong over the last four jumps letting Ella gain speed as if we were flying.

Red and Barbara were waiting at the finish line. Red looked at me asking, "how did it go?" as I was bring Ella to a complete halt. I looked at her with a grin telling her we had gone over every fence without taking any faults. Barbara gave me a high five. Our team was now in the hunt for a ribbon.

We all walked Ella out, loosening her girth to let her cool down from her strenuous run. I brought her up to the horse trough where she proceeded to dunk her whole head in the water, swishing it back and forth, splashing water everywhere, cooling not only herself down but me along with her. After talking with my teammates, I started walking back to Ella's stall. I was tired, and if I was tired I thought that Ella had to be spent. I gave her a good rub-down and led her to the sandy beach that ran along the end of the grounds. I wanted to be alone to think over what had happened that day. As soon as we hit the sandy beach she layed down and rolled giving her body a good rub down. After she was finished she stood up quickly and shook the sand from her beautiful coat. I jumped up onto her back and walked her into the water up past her knees. I expected her to paw at the water and play but she just stood there perfectly still looking out over the water with all her attention on something unseen. It was if she knew that something was coming up and she had to be ready for it. I leaned forward on her and placed my arms around her neck as the water gently lapped over her legs. At that moment our hearts were truly joined. The moment passed and I took her over to a nice patch of green grass to let her graze and dry off.

As I grazed her I talked to her about what lay ahead. While I stroked her smooth glossy coat I told her we had to pass the vet check in the morning with no signs of lameness so we could do the show jumping portion of the competition. I promised to memorize my course and keep her safe. She twitched her ears listening as I talked to her, telling her how wonderful she was and all that she meant to me. The next day was weighing heavily on me. I knew the course was going to be challenging and I would had given anything to talk with Brad about all this anxiety I had building up in me. He always knew how to get me to loosen up before I would turn myself into a ball of nerves.

As I was walking back to the stall I heard someone come up beside me and whisper, "Don't look. Just focus on you and Ella and the job before you." I turned around, and there was Brad. Carol was standing right beside him. I squealed and gave them each a huge hug.

The next day was just plain hot and uncomfortable. We had fans on the front of each horse's stall to keep them as cool as possible. We fed the horses and got ready for the vet check.

Nerves were running high. I knew we were doing well and that just added to the pressure. We were all unusually quiet.

At Event competitions I always stayed away from the scoreboard. I really did not want to know the scores. I already knew we were competing against the best riders that the country had to offer, and I had to ride my best no matter what that board said.

Now Red on the other hand, did not just know her scores, but everyone else's in the competition. She had figured every possible scenario of how we could win. She had it down to how many rails could be pulled and still stay in the running.

I covered my ears, yelling "No, stop, I don't want to know," as she rattled on and on with all her different scenarios and each horse's weakness.

I finally took a bucket of water and threw it at her to make her stop. She grabbed the hose and turned it on me as I dove behind Rebecca and Barbara. Well, that started it. For the next couple of minutes the water fight was on. We were all laughing so hard our sides hurt.

I looked up and there stood our coach with her hands on her hips, shaking her head. All she said is, "You have one half hour to clean up this mess and get yourselves over to the arena for the walk through."

That water fight had completely taken my mind off the pressure, and I felt like we as a team could do this. We walked the course and talked about how each horse was to take the jumps. Thanks to Red, I knew we could knock three rails off the jumps and still be in the running. I memorized the course and the coach had me repeat it to everyone else on the team just to make sure I did not forget it.

We went back to saddle up the horses. This was it! All the time and training I had done was now coming down to this last course. I whispered a little prayer and mounted Ella knowing she would not let me down.

I would be the last person on our team to ride the course. Red was first to go. She had a good ride going but came into the last jump too strong and knocked a rail down. We now only had the cushion of two rails. Barbara was next; her horse looked tired during her warm up and I held my breath as she entered the ring and started her course. It was slow and she had a few close calls, but she went clean. I breathed deeply. We still had a two-rail padding. Next was Rebecca, our most experienced rider at this level. I could see that both she and her horse were worn out; the heat was taking its toll. I watched as she did her courtesy circle. She had good cadence and made the first set of jumps without a problem. I took a breath. As she came into a triple jump I knew she did not have enough impulsion to make it through clean. She pulled two rails. As she came to the last jump, her horse took a wrong step and pulled another rail. There was no cushion left. Ella and I had to go clean to tie for first place.

As I was waiting my turn I watched the other riders jump their rounds. Some were having a hard time. The heat was really taking a toll on them. Three riders pulled rails down, and one had a refusal. I was really beginning to feel the pressure.

There was one rider ahead of me when I closed my eyes, visualizing each jump, and seeing Ella clearing each fence with room to spare. Just as I was going into the arena, Red laid her hand on me and said, "If you go clean, we can tie for first." I looked at her and just said, "Thanks, Red. I will do my best." As I cantered past her to do my courtesy circle, she said, "Don't forget to breathe." What would I do without Red? No matter the situation, she made me laugh.

Ella felt relaxed and strong under me as we took the first fence. She knew her business and her confidence helped me focus right to the last fence. We went clean. We were now tied for first place and there would have to be a tie breaker.

Rebecca, as the captain of the team, was expected to ride the tie breaker. She also had the option of giving it to another team member. I saw her talking to the coach and did not think much about it. I knew she would never pick me. She never let me forget my faults. I slipped off Ella and was loosening her girth, getting ready to watch the tie breaker.

From behind me I heard my name called. "Nicole," Rebecca said.

I just stared at her and couldn't believe she had called me by my real name. I had not thought that she even knew my real name.

"Nicole," she said again as she patted Ella. I want you to ride the tie breaker. I couldn't take it in. I just looked at her and narrowed my eyes. She continued, "my horse is exhausted; the heat has exhausted him. Ella's the best horse here and is our best hope to win." Everything in me wanted to say no. All the years of jabs and backbiting marched in front of me and the stubborn streak inside of me started to rise up. Red was watching our exchange and could see me stiffen. She knew there was bad blood between us and decided to step in saying,

"Now, now. Live and let live. Shake hands and let the past go. I want to win this thing."

I looked at Red, shook my head, and said, "Have you no humility at all?"

She replied, "No, none at all. Now shake hands."

Rebecca put her hand out. I looked at it, shook my head, and took it, saying "You can call me Charity." It felt good to let go of all that anger.

As I watched the course be reset for the next round I grew very nervous. The jumps looked beyond Ella's ability. The jumps were so much bigger and wider than anything we had ever jumped. I knew that if I wanted to do this there could be no mistakes.

I handed Ella to Red and asked her to hold her while I walked the course. Rebecca came into the arena with me and we talked about each jump and about the best way to shave time off without taking rails. I was surprised at how well she knew Ella and told her so.

She replied, "You have always been my stiffest competition and I have studied your horse for years."

"You surprise me, Rebecca," was all I could say as we walked out of the arena to get Ella ready for this timed jump off.

I mounted Ella and she could feel that I was tense. I had broken out in a cold sweat. My heart was pounding and I'm sure Ella could feel the tenseness throughout my whole body. She started sidestepping when I got her into the ring. I couldn't get her to hold still. I saluted my judge, and the whistle blew. Ella leaped forward like a bullet. I knew I had to have complete control in order to go clean with the better time. If she didn't listen to me we would not do well. I circled her in front of the start flags. Then I crossed the start line. Control and speed is what I needed right then. She had the speed, but control was another issue. We were practically flying. We soared over the first fence with barely any room to spare. I kept trying to bring her back to me. We soared over the second fence and then approached the combination that led to a fence that had a sharp turn. We had to make that turn. At that speed I wasn't sure we would. I sat back and pulled and turned, hoping she would follow my body and she did! She knew what she was doing. We whipped over the next four fences faster than we had ever done before. I heard the roar of the crowd as I flew past the finish line. Dirt flying up from under Ella's heels. I pulled Ella up and looked at our time. It was good. We had done our best and just had to wait and see if it was enough.

I watched the other rider go into the arena. His horse was feeling the pressure and was so wound up he gave a buck. Once he got his horse under control the whistle blew, and he was on his way. His speed was incredible. He was going much faster than Ella had gone. *If he keeps this speed and goes clean he'll beat me*, I thought. As he came to the fifth fence, which had a sharp rollback, his horse was going too fast to make the turn, and he missed the fence completely.

I couldn't believe it. We had just won. I was shocked. I wrapped my arms around this wonderful horse with such a big heart. I had unchecked tears running down my cheeks. We had gone through so much work to get here. My teammates were congratulating me by pulling me off Ella and dumping a bucket of water over me. Carol, Klaus, and Brad came running up; they were so happy. Carol had tears in her eyes. Everyone was saying, "Congratulations!" Lucy, Frank and grandma took Ella from me to cool her down. My dad gave me a big bear hug telling me how proud of me he was. My mother stood at a distance with a look of astonishment on her face. I don't think she quite knew what to think. I grabbed her hand telling her how pleased I was that she had come. She had seen Ella give me all she had to give. She got to see us as a team.

Now Ella is gone and my life will never be the same. Tears were splashing down on the picture I was holding of the little girl holding the tiny foal in her arms.

Epilogue

*E*veryone in our Club knew that I needed to sell Ella before I was to go off to college. There was a new girl in our club named Terry that was looking for an upper level horse and she had her eye on Ella. She was a good rider and I knew she would be good to Ella. They only lived a few miles down the road from the Equestrian Center so I could see her anytime I wanted.

A few weeks after the show Terry's dad overheard my mother talking about Ella to the owner of the small grocery store that was across from our house. He introduced himself telling her all about his daughter and the small farm they had just down the road. He said he would be very interested in buying Ella and offered a very fair price for her.

That night My mom and dad sat me down and said selling Ella was the only thing to do. Not only would it send me through college, but it would also help my sister. I could not believe they wanted me to do this. I did not care if I went to college, but my sister's needs were the thing my parents used to get me to agree.

A week after I had said goodbye to Ella, Brad found her standing in the driveway of the Equestrian Center looking around as if she had lost something. He walked up to her gently placing a rope over her head saying, "I miss her too. Come on we need to call your owner and let them know we found you."

He called Bob saying he found Ella and that he must have left a gate open. No, Bob was certain that all gates had been closed. All the rest of his horses were safe in the pasture but he would check just the same to make sure.

The next day Ella was found in Frank's pasture grazing with Dusty and Rebel. That is how it went the rest of the week. Bob would put the horses out in the morning making sure all the gates were closed and the horses were safe in the pasture. Sometime during the morning Ella must have jumped the fence, made her way to Frank's jumping his fence and made herself at home. No one told me that this was going on. They just hoped she would quit doing this sometime soon.

That weekend I came home for a visit from school. I had planned on sleeping late but was awakened by my mother loudly calling to my father to come quickly. I came out to see what was going on. Grandma was standing with a grin on her face. They were all looking out into the back yard.

"What is going on?" I asked.

"Someone has come for a visit," grandma said.

I looked out into the back yard and there stood Ella grazing under our large willow tree. I slid the sliding glass door open to the back yard and quietly called Ella's name. Her head came up nickering to me as she walked toward me. She buried her beautiful head into my chest gently nudging me. I stroked her beautiful neck as she asked for her sweet spot to be rubbed.

Frank came running into the yard saying, "I thought that I saw her gallop through the back yard."

My mother looked at my dad and said, "you have to call Bob and let him know that we just can't sell this horse. She won't let us."

Frank told me the whole story while my dad was on the phone with Bob.

Dad came back from the phone call saying that Bob understood and there would be no problem getting the horse back. "We had quite a conversation about horses. He really knows his stuff. He just really admires Ella's loyalty and was wondering while you were busy with school if he could have a baby from her. I said I would ask you. It would really help with your schooling costs," he said looking at my mother.

Frank was offering to keep Ella at his farm. He reassured me that he and Lucy would take good care of her while I was at school.

My head was spinning and I could hardly take in all that was happening; everyone was talking at once. The one thing I did understand was my Ella was coming back to me. The words of my mother softly rose within me as I put my arms around Ella's neck; "When God shuts a door, he always opens a window."

Glossary of Equestrian Terms

Balance: The horse is carrying the riders and its own weight in the most efficient way. The weight is on the hind legs (the quarters) not on the front legs (the forehand).

Bowed tendon: An inflammation and enlargement of the flexor tendon at the back of the cannon (most often found on the front legs).

Collection: This is a state in which the horse is gathered together. As he engages his hindquarters, his hind legs bend more in every joint and carry more weight. His balance shifts to the rear, and his back and neck rise, making his forehand lighter. His steps become shorter, and elevated, and elastic, and he moves with lightness and energy.

Cross Country Jumping: Cross country jumping is a test of endurance, skill and agility following a prescribed course through forest and fields. The horse and rider are required to negotiate natural obstacles like logs, ditches, streams, banks, hills, and fences. The course may be over 2 miles.

Dressage: Exercise and training that develops the physique and ability of the horse. The object of Dressage is the harmonious development of the physique and ability of the horse. As a result it makes the horse calm, supple, loose and flexible but also confident, attentive and keen, thus achieving perfect understanding with his rider.

Eventing: (also known as horse trials) is an equestrian event where a single horse and rider combination compete against other combinations across the three disciplines of dressage, cross-country, and show jumping. This event has its roots in a comprehensive cavalry test requiring mastery of several types of riding.

Farrier: A fully qualified and professional horse shoe fitter.

Filly: A young female horse under four years old.

Foal: A young or newborn horse, either male or female, up to yearling age.

Grooming: Removal of dirt and other irritants from the horse. Grooming massages your horse's muscles and helps build up a personal relationship, akin to pairing up between two horses in a field.

Half halt: A method of bringing the horse to a greater degree of balance and higher mental attention.

Hand: the unit by which the height of a horse is measured. A hand equals 4 inches.

Longe Line: A long line, about 20 to 30 feet, used to train and exercise a horse.

Lightness: When a horse moves with impulsion, suppleness, and the right degree of self-carriage, he is light: athletic, and able to move in any gait or direction at the slightest indication. Lightness is highly dependent on good riding and on harmony between horse and rider.

Show Jumping: Competitive equestrian event in which horse and rider are required to jump, usually within a time limit, a series of obstacles that have been designed for a particular show.

Tack: Riding equipment or gear for the horse such as saddle, bridle, halter, and so forth.

9 781545 624777